"Unseen Footsteps of Jesus"

OLAM HABA

(Future World)

Mysteries Book 2-"The Dawning"

Jerry Ayers

authorHOUSE

AuthorHouse™
1663 Liberty Drive
Bloomington, IN 47403
www.authorhouse.com
Phone: 833-262-8899

© 2023 Jerry Ayers. All rights reserved.

No part of this book may be reproduced, stored in a retrieval system, or transmitted by any means without the written permission of the author.

Published by AuthorHouse 02/01/2023

ISBN: 978-1-7283-7810-7 (sc)
ISBN: 978-1-7283-7808-4 (hc)
ISBN: 978-1-7283-7809-1 (e)

Library of Congress Control Number: 2023901775

Print information available on the last page.

Any people depicted in stock imagery provided by Getty Images are models, and such images are being used for illustrative purposes only.
Certain stock imagery © Getty Images.

This book is printed on acid-free paper.

Because of the dynamic nature of the Internet, any web addresses or links contained in this book may have changed since publication and may no longer be valid. The views expressed in this work are solely those of the author and do not necessarily reflect the views of the publisher, and the publisher hereby disclaims any responsibility for them.

CONTENTS

Chapter 1 1
Chapter 2 13
Chapter 3 26
Chapter 4 39
Chapter 5 52
Chapter 6 67
Chapter 7 77
Chapter 8 89
Chapter 9 101
Chapter 10 114
Chapter 11 126
Chapter 12 141

1

....Miss Nanny goat quickly bolted through the open wooden door and scampered towards the house bleating and shaking her head. Back in the wooden goat shed the body of fifteen-year old Miryam (Mary) began to stir ever so slowly. She could hear a faint voice calling her name, "Miryam, Miryam." Her body seemed numb but her mind was racing with unanswered questions. *"Where am I?" "What has happened to me?" "Who keeps calling my name and why?" "Am I dreaming?"* As she began to come to her senses the answers to her questions came ever so slowly. She laid motionless on the dusty and straw covered floor of the goat shed for an eternity it seemed. She opened her eyes slowly and a blurred image of the brown thatched roof came into focus. The rough pole beams and dried palm tree branches hovered above her as she felt weak and disorientated. *"There's that voice again. What does it want?"* thought Miryam. "Miryam. Miryam girl why don't you answer me?" the voice demanded.

Miryam could hear heavy footsteps nearing her accompanied by low grunting and a dragging sound through the dry grass. Before she could gather her wits to sit up, there was suddenly peering down at her a horned beast with a pair of beady eyes, two flaring nostrils and a long white beard. Then came the weathered brown round face of cook towering just above the beast. "Miss Nanny was up to the house making a buffet of my lotus and marigolds!" scolded cook shaking her crooked index finger on her free hand. Miss Nanny let out a loud bleat as cook continued her scolding, "Girl, what are you doing? It is

1

almost dark, supper is getting cold, *Chanukah,* Hanukkah service is in two hours, Miss Nanny is running loose and you are taking a nap! Speak to me girl, you look a fright." Miryam stammered, "I…I…don't know for sure. One minute I was trying to milk Miss Nanny and then the next….the messenger angel…the heavy gust of wind…you standing over me…" Cook butted in, "*Oy vey,* oh pain, love sick I tell ya', just plain love sick. Ain't no carpenter boy gonna fancy a crumpled mess like you now. Hurry up to the house and get cleaned up before your grandfather finds out what you have been doing. Good thing you got a bucket of milk or we both would be in a fix. Now give me your hand." Miryam extended her hand and cook gave a mighty tug as Miryam seemed to fly to her feet. "Thanks cook," Miryam replied brushing the dust and straw off her dress. Cook sternly said, "Now hurry up and take the milk to the house and get cleaned up for service. I will finish tending to Miss Nanny. Don't let your uncle Yowceph (Joseph) or your sister Shalowmit (Salome) catch you or you will have questions to answer. Now get going."

Miryam scampered across the backyard to the house taking great care not to spill any of the milk from the bucket. Once safely inside the house she sat the bucket in the kitchen and softly tip-toed to her room after removing her sandals. She could hear the voices of her grandfather, uncle and sister in the other part of the house. As she opened her bedroom door ever so slowly the old hinges let out a groaning creak sound but not too loud, she hoped. Miryam only opened the door so that the opening was just wide enough for her to slip inside sideways not allowing the door hinges to announce her entrance. Once safely inside she quietly shut the door and sighed a deep sigh of relief. She very quickly changed her clothes and adorned herself a little extra for the *Chanukah,* Hanukkah service but doing it rapidly paying close attention to detail. Then she swung the door open to make her grand entrance as the bedroom door hinges let out a high pitched squeal as if to trumpet her appearance in front of her audience.

When she appeared in the doorway of the great room Miryam let out a loud, "Uh-hum. How do I look?" The conversation stopped and all three heads looked her way and thirteen-year old Shalowmit (Salome) quipped, "I don't know why you spent all that time getting ready for service, next year I am going to stay and help you so you don't take so long!" Next ten-year old Yowceph expressed his dissatisfaction of the long delay waiting for his older niece, "Besides, I am starving. I think my stomach has already eaten a hole in my good worship robe!" Miryam being quick witted quipped, "Yowceph that is so that your worship clothing is Holy." All four of them burst out into uncontrolled laughter which was only interrupted by cook calling them to the evening meal. Miryam thought to herself as they walked to the dining parlor, *"Whew! That was a close call. I will tell grandfather what really happened after service tonight. He will understand."*

Just a few hours prior to this far, far-away to the East on that same day in the year of 5 B.C, in the great city of Babel (Babylon-modern Iraq) gathered the most powerful sages known in the East. They were known in their native tongue as Magi, holy priests of the Zoroastrain religion. A single priest was known as a Mag and the addition of the letter 'i' made it plural Magi. They were very skilled in the arts of magic and astrology. What made these five Magi unique was that their ancestors were heavily influenced by the Hebrew priests during the seventy years of captivity of the Hebrew people by King Nbuwkadne'tstsar (Nebuchadnezzar) king of the territory of Mesopotamia. Therefore, they also followed the astrology of the Hebrew people and the story of Yahuah. They had gathered in the city of Babel because of the great growing light in the night sky.

Those gathered from the country of Babel (Babylon-modern Iraq) were: Nbuwzaradan from the town of Opis; Kadashman from the town of Sippar; Belsha'tstsar from the town of Nippur; Zabaia from the town of Erech; and Hammurabi from the great city of Babel. Also, gathered with them were their personal apprentices, so tonight would be a night of great teaching.

Hammurabi, the great teacher, opened the small gathering under the stars by quoting the Hebrew Thillah (Psalm) 19:1-4. He raised both arms toward the twinkling stars of the night sky and said, "**The heavens are telling the story of Yahuah and their expanse is declaring the work of His hands. Day to day pours forth speech and night to night reveals knowledge. There is no speech nor are there words. Their voice is not heard. Their line has gone out through all the earth and their utterances to the end of the world. In them He has placed a tent for the sun.**" Hammurabi continued, "Before we get started into our night-watching this evening, let us review the basics of the story of night-watching as told by the ancestors of the Hebrews. I would like each of the Magi to have their apprentice share in the story telling from the beginning."

Mag Nbuwzaradan from the town of Opis said to his apprentice, "Shadrak, you get to start with the easy one. Explain what the Hellene (Greek) word 'zodiac' means." Shadrak jumped to his feet and said, "It is made of two words. The fist word is *zoe* and it means 'life' which is followed by the second word of *dia* meaning pathway. Therefore zodiac means 'the path to life'." Mag Nbuwzaradan smiled from ear to ear as Mag Hammurabi said, "Well done young Shadrak, you may be seated." Next Mag Kadashman from the town of Sippar said to his apprentice, "Meyshak, what do you know about the Hebrew constellation of *Ariy* (Leo the lion)." Meyshak unfolded his little legs and stood erect and said, "*Ariy* in the Hebrew language means a lion but we call it *Asad*. The Hellene and Romans call it Leo. We know that the lion has a very bright star between his front feet which is the handle or scepter of a sickle that comes out of the lion's mouth. The word feet in Hebrew is *"regal*eo' or regal leo. We call that star *Qalb al-Asad* meaning 'heart of lion'. The Hellene and Romans call the star 'regulus'." Mag Hammurabi exclaimed, "Excellent, excellent young Meyshak! However, before you sit down what do the ancient Hebrews say about this lion constellation with its bright star and please quote your reference." Meyshak took a deep breath and said, "According to the Hebrew book of Bre'shiyth (Genesis) 49:9-10 **'Yhuwdah (Judah) is a lion's whelp. From the prey my son you have gone up. He crouches, he lies down like a lion and as a lion who dares rouse him up. The scepter shall not depart from Yhuwdah (Judah) nor the ruler's staff from between his feet until Shiyloh (Shiloh) comes And to Him shall be the obedience of the peoples'.** Oh yeah, Shiyloh in the Hebrew tongue means "Prince of Peace". When young Meyshak had finished all clapped their hands and he sat down once again.

Then Mag Belsha'tstsar from the town of Nippur addressed his apprentice, "Abed Ngow please stand and tell us about the Hebrew constellation of *Dagyim* (Pisces the fish)" Abed Ngow puffed out his chest and clearly stated, "The Hebrew *Dagyim* means 'more than one fish' and is the same as the Hellene (Greek) and Roman Pisces. The ancient Hebrew tradition claims that this constellation represents the house of Yisra'Yah (Israel)." Mag Hammurabi said, "Stated to perfection young Abed Ngow. You may be seated" Next, Mag Zabaia from the town of Erech directed his young apprentice to stand up and said, "Ok, Gungunam give us your knowledge of the third and the fourth constellations that we watch." Gungunam was the oldest of the apprentices at the age of twelve. He was gangly and as thin as a beanpole but loved to learn. Gungunam closed his eyes and began to speak, "The third is known in the Hebrew tongue as *Bethuwlah* meaning 'virgin' but the Hellene (Greek) call it 'Parthenos' and the Romans call it Virgo. The fourth is known in the Hebrew tongue as Akrab meaning scorpion or conflict. The ancient Hebrew teachers represent this constellation as Satan. The Hellene and Romans call it Scorpius or Scorpio for short." Mag Hammurabi commented, "Young Gungunam you have gotten wiser as you age. You may be seated." Then Mag Hammurabi put his hand above his eyes on his forehead as if looking for something and said, "Who has not participated in this teaching review? I know he is here but I don't see him."

At that comment little seven-year old Marduk raised his hand and waved it frantically. Mag Hammurabi loved teasing the youngest apprentice even if it was his own apprentice. Mag Hammurabi continued the teasing and said, "Would the last young man please stand up because I can't see you." The rest of the apprentices giggled and the Magi began to laugh as little Marduk jumped up and down appearing to have hit a bee hive. "Oh there you are young Marduk would you please tell us about the chief star that we watch?" asked Mag Hammurabi. Marduk smiled a big smile and replied, "The chief star is known in the Hebrew tongue as *Shabbethay* meaning 'restful'. The Hellene (Greek) refer to it as Cronus and the Romans call it Saturn. The ancient Hebrew teachers state that Saturn is representative of the first king of the Universe whose name was *Adam*. "Before Mag Hammurabi could say anything young Marduk took a bow which once again brought laughter. Then Mag Hammurabi said, "Fine, fine job young Marduk. Please sit down."

Mag Nbuwzaradan of Opis called upon his apprentice Shadrak once again, "Shadrak tell us about another star that we watch." Shadrak stood to his feet and said, "I want to talk about the star in the Hebrew tongue called *Tsadaq* meaning 'righteous'. The ancients speak of a new King of the Universe coming one day which is represented by the star *Tsadaq*. The Hellene call the star Zeus and the Romans call it Jupiter." Next Mag Kadashman of Sippar showcased his apprentice Meyshak saying, "Your turn to choose a star that we watch." Meyshak came to his feet and said, "I will talk about the star in the native Hebrew tongue called *Nogah* meaning 'very bright light'. The Hebrew people refer to this star as the *Melehut haShamayim* meaning "Queen of Heaven". Their prophet Yirmyah (Jeremiah) who had spent some time in our land during their captivity, said in his book chapter 7:18 **'The sons gather wood and the fathers kindle the fire and the women kneed swelling fermented dough to make round ash-cakes for the Queen of the lofty sky where the clouds move and to pour out drink offerings to elohiym false pagan god idols that they may trouble Me with grief and rage.'** The Hellene (Greek) call this same star Aphrodite, the Romans call it Venus and we call it here in Babylon Astarte."

Not to be outdone Belsha'tstsar of Nippur called upon his apprentice Abed Ngow, "Abed Ngow which of the two remaining stars do you wish to tell us about?" Abed Ngow who had already stood up at his master's gesture said, "I think I want to share with you about the star in the native Hebrew language known as *Tsayar* meaning 'messenger'. The Hellene call it Hermes and the Romans call it Mercury." Then Zabaia of Erech said to Gungunam his apprentice, "You have the last one. Do you know it?" Gungunam replied, "Yes, sir. The last of the stars that we watch is known in the Hebrew tongue as *Milchamah* meaning 'war'. The Hellene call the star Ares and the Romans call it Mars." Then little Marduk jumped up eager to respond to his master Mag Hammurabi. Mag Hammurabi said, "I am sorry Marduk but there aren't any more stars. We are done." Then Marduk pouted and stuck out his bottom lip. Then he exclaimed, "I know, I can tell the beginning story." Mag Hammurabi said, "No little Marduk. I am glad you are eager but the story is much too hard for a little boy like you. However, I will let you give it a try."

Little Marduk stood as tall as he could and began, "Over 4,000 years ago according to the ancient Hebrew peoples, their god Yahuah created the constellations and the stars. At that time, in the beginning, *Shabbethay* (Saturn) the first Adam, was in the paws of the constellation of *Ariy* (Leo Lion) near the bright star *Regaleo* (Regulus) ruling the Universe. By the star *Shemesh* (Sun) were the stars *Yareach* (Moon), *Milchamah* (Mars), *Tsayar* (Mercury) and *Nogah* (Venus). *Tsadaq* (Jupiter) was in the consolation of *Dagyim* (Pisces the Fish). Then *Nogah* (Venus) joined *Shabbethay* (Saturn) in the constellation *Ariy* (Leo Lion). While *Shabbethay* (Saturn) was ruling the Universe *Nogah* (Venus) wandered out of the paws of *Ariy* (Leo Lion) and ran towards the constellation of *Nachash* (Scorpio Serpent Scorpion). When *Nogah* (Venus) entered into *Nachash* (Scorpio Serpent Scorpion) *Shabbethay* (Saturn) ran after her and joined her in *Nachash* (Scorpio Serpent Scorpion). Then *Shemesh* (Sun) and *Milchamah* (Mars) joined them inside *Nachash* (Scorpio Serpent Scorpion)."

Marduk continued, "The Hebrew prophet Mosheh (Moses) told of this in the book of Bre'shiyth 'In the Beginning' chapter 3:14-15, **'So Yahuah Yah said to Nachash (Serpent) because you have done this, cursed are you above all the livestock and all the wild animals! You will crawl on your belly and you will eat dust all the days of your life. I will put Milchamah (Mars-war) between you and the woman Nogah (Venus) and between her offspring and hers. He will crush your head and you will strike his heel.'** Then *Shabbethay* (Saturn), the first Adam and *Nogah* (Venus) left *Nachash (*Scorpio Serpent Scorpion) followed by *Shemesh* (Sun) and *Milchamah* (Mars). As *Shemesh* (Sun) left, then

Tsadaq (Jupiter) left the constellation *Dagyim* (Pisces the Fish). This was explained in the Hebrew book of *Bamidbar* meaning 'In the desert Wilderness' (Exodus) 24:9, 17 **'Like a lion they crouch and lie down. Like a lioness who dares to rouse them? I see him but not now; I behold him but not near. A star will come out of Yisra'Yah (Israel) [Pisces] a scepter [Regaleo]** (Regulus) **will rise out of Yisra'Yah [Leo]'**

Mardjuk explained further, *"Tsadaq the Righteous* (Jupiter) came out of the pair of fish to replace the first Adam *Shabbethay* (Saturn) as a new King of the Universe. Then according to the ancients on today's calendar of Caesar, May 5, 3502 B.C. *Shabbethay Adam* (Saturn) returned near the *Regaleo* (Regulus) star in the paws of *Ariy* (Leo Lion) and then left. Next on the same calendar on August 1, 3502 *Tsadaq Righteousness* the New King of the Universe joined the star *Regaleo* (Regulus) in the paws of *Ariiy* (Leo Lion) and left. Finally, on June 27, 3501 B.C. *Regaleo* (Regulus) the ruling scepter in the paws of *Ariy* (Leo Lion) was joined by both *Shabbethay Adam* (Saturn) and *Tsadaq Righteous* (Jupiter) the New King of the Universe and united in one bright light." Mag Hammurabi and the rest of the Magi and apprentices were stunned in silence. Finally, he stuttered, "How did you…where did you…..who did you learn that from?" "From you master Hammurabi. You go over that story every time we are getting ready for the dark to let the stars shine each evening," replied Marduk. "But you are never paying any attention as we walk. You are always picking up rocks or bugs or chasing something!" stated Mag Hammurabi. In defense little Marduk replied, "Yes, sire but I do pay attention too!" At that the Magi ruffled the hair of the little boy and sat down for the teaching of the Master of Magi as Hammurabi prepared for the night-watching.

Mag Hammurabi began, "Brother Magi, we have gathered here because not too many years ago the night sky began to brighten with an unknown light. Then six months ago to this very day the star *Tsayar Messenger* (Mercury) and *Nogah* (Venus) dashed into the belly of *Ariy* (Leo Lion). This can only mean that a messenger was being prepared to be born in the Hebrew nation of Yhuwdah (Judah). We also know that *Shemesh* (Sun) has entered into the constellation *Bethuwah the Virgin* (Virgo). Therefore, that is why we are watching the night sky to see who and what the message is about….." Hammurabi was interrupted by a bright light running across the night sky. The Magi looked up and watched as *Nogah* (Venus) made a mad dash to join *Shemesh* (Sun) in the constellation of *Bethuwah the Virgin* (Virgo) followed rapidly by *Tsayar Messenger* (Mercury). Then a short time later *Tsayar Messenger* (Merrcury) left the constellation but was quickly replaced by a rapid moving stream of light coming from *Tsadaq Righteous* (Jupiter). Next *Tsadaq Righteous* and *Nogah* (Venus) moved to the matrix abdomen and rested with *Shemesh* (Sun-Yahuah) hovering above them.

The Magi began contemplating among themselves to the meaning of the latest activity of the stars in the constellations. One had one idea and another had a different idea. All five Magi could not agree on the light show that Yahuah had just provided for them. What story was the sky telling? After a couple hours of discussion all the apprentices had drifted off to sleep from the mundane arguing except little Marduk. He went to his master and tugged on his robe only to get brushed off. So he tried to get the attention of one of the other Magi by tapping on their arms or sides. Finally, he could not stand it anymore and yelled, "Excuse me anointed Magi of the East!" The heated discussions ceased and all eyes were upon little Marduk in surprise. Marduk continued, "My masters have not mentioned the Hebrew prophecy in the book of Ysha'Yah (Isaiah) 7:14, **'Therefore, Yahuah Himself will give you a sign. The virgin will be with child**

and will give birth to a son and will call Him, Immanu'Yah, which means Yahuah with us.' I think the New King of the Universe has been picked by Yahuah Himself and with the 'messenger' showing up twice in two constellations, it will probably happen very soon. Also, tonight is the Hebrew celebration of *Chanukah*, Hanukkah which is the Festival of Lights." The Magi looked at each other and then back to the boy with astonishment and said, "The boy has a point Mag Hammurabi. We believe we should remain in Babel (Babylon-modern Iraq) with you until the show is over."

Miryam (Mary), her sister Shalowmit (Salome) and cook walked behind their grandfather, Matityahu ben Levi and their little uncle Yowceph trying not to get too much dust in their sandals before they entered the synagogue for the special service tonight. As Miryam looked up the stars seemed to dance with the moon in the evening sky. As they entered into the synagogue Miryam followed cook and Shalowmit (Salome) up the stairs to the women and children's gallery while her uncle Yowceph and grandfather Matityahu ben Levi joined Ya'aqob (Jacob) ben El'azar and her proposed husband Yowceph. Then her mind began to wander on the events of the day. Thoughts once again raced through her head, *'Was it real or just a dream?' 'If it was real why would Yahuah choose me anyway?' 'But I could really hear the booming voice and that bright light hurt my eyes.' 'What about that bucket of milk? I didn't milk Miss Nanny so who did?'* A sharp pain in her side brought her back to the present in the synagogue. It was the long boney finger of cook jabbing her in the side prompting her as it was time to go. "Oiy, veh! (oh pain) You poor lovesick bird, I bet ya didn't even hear the sermon or your love Yowceph read the scripture tonight did you?" nagged the cook. Miryam quipped back, "Yes, I did. He read a portion from the Towrah (Torah)!" Cook rolled her eyes as Miryam (Mary) scampered down the stairs to catch up with her grandfather.

When they got back to the house everyone headed towards their bedroom saying good-night except Miryam lingered to visit with her grandfather. After Matityahu ben Levi threw the last log on the fire in the fireplace Miryam sat down by him leaning on his side. "What is it my dear granddaughter?" asked Matityahu ben Levi. Miryam (Mary) began to pour out all that was on her troubled mind, "Oh grandfather, I have something to tell you. As you know before the evening meal I went out back to milk Miss Nanny and was delayed coming into the parlor. Well, what you don't know is that during the normal tussle with Miss Nanny a messenger angel from Yahuah came to visit me in the barn. He said that I was going to become pregnant by the Sacred Breath of Yahuah and bear a son who will rule the nations to the Messianic Period and then a big gust of wind knocked me to the floor. There was this bright cloud surrounding me and ..."

Matityahu ben Levi had heard enough and sternly reproached her saying, "That is blasphemy granddaughter and even treason against Rome and Herod. I am sure you just hit your head in the tussle and don't have your wits about you. Don't you ever mention this again!" Miryam (Mary) began to protest but her grandfather cut her off quickly, "Don't you know that if you are pregnant that you will be stoned to death and if Yowceph did this to you he will be required to pay fifty shekels of silver to me!" Miryam (Mary) burst into tears, "The angel even told me that Aunt Elysheba (Elizabeth) is even now in her sixth month!" This put Matityahu over the edge and he yelled, "Nonsense, your aunt Elysheba (Elizabeth) is old and barren. Now get to bed and don't ever speak of this matter again! Do you hear me child?" Miryam quickly trotted to her room sobbing and slammed her wooden bedroom door vibrating the rest of the house. Shalowmit (Salome) sat straight up in bed and stared with wide open eyes at her sobbing and trembling sister Miryam (Mary).

2

The next morning at the breakfast table, Miryam (Mary) could feel that the tension from the previous night still existed. All eyes were looking at her, and when she would look back they would quickly look down at their plates again, except for her grandfather. The air was normally filled with lively chatter but this morning she was met with silence and the sound of goblets clanking back on the table after their liquid contents had soothed the throats of their users. Even cook who usually stood over the brood and putting her two cents into the conversations, when she felt it was needed, was absent. She would make rushed dashes to the table and then return just as quickly back to the kitchen. Then finally the silence was broken as Miryam (Mary) tried to put her best foot forward after she finished a mouthful of food.

"Grandfather, about last night......" she began but was quickly cut off. Matityahu ben Levi chimed in, "*Ken, ken*, Yes yes, about last night. I have been doing some thinking on that subject after you mentioned your Aunt Elysheba (Elizabeth), the poor old woman. As you know *Pecach*, Passover, is just three months away and your Uncle Zkaryah (Zechariah) will be required to be in Yruwshalaim (Jerusalem) to serve in the Temple. She has a lot of work to be done before that time arrives so I feel it would be best if you would go and give your aunt a much needed hand. However, I will send instructions that you must return before *Pecach*, Passover so that you will be home for the celebration here. I have prepared everything this morning. The donkeys are loaded except for your personal needs and I have hired two body guards to accompany you there. I would love to go myself but I have much pressing business matters concerning the mining business that must be attended to. You will depart directly after you finish your breakfast."

"*So that's, that,*" Miryam (Mary) thought, "*no more discussion, no reasoning, just send the crazy girl away and hope she comes home with her senses about her.*" Miryam replied, "*Ken*, yes, grandfather. I know Aunt Elysheba will be extremely happy to see me. *Pecach*, Passover, will be very special this year and we have a lot of work to do. I will go to my room and collect my personal things." At that she excused herself from the table and went to her bedroom to start packing for the trip. As she gathered her things she silently prayed, "*Oh Yahuah, You are all knowing and I trust you with my very breath. You have a reason that I must depart and leave my family and future husband Yowceph (Joseph) during this exciting and wonderful time of my life. I am your servant and will not question your will. My only prayer is that my thoughts be Your thoughts and my actions be Your actions. May the peace that you have given me flow to my grandfather as he is a righteous man. In Your loving Name of Yahuah, I pray this prayer. Halal Yah* (Celebrate and shed the light of Yahuah)."

Then Miryam (Mary) lifted the satchel of extra cloths and personal things off her straw mattress and went out her bedroom door. Once again the wooden door hinges groaned and shrieked as she opened and closed the door behind her. When she looked up she could see, cook, her grandfather, young uncle Yowceph (Joseph) and her sister Shalowmit (Salome) waiting by the front door. She forced herself to smile as she made her way to the front door. Cook was the first to greet her with a bear hug, "Tell your Aunt Elysheba *shalom* (peace, happiness, good health, prosperity) for me." Then it was her young uncle Yowceph (Joseph), "Here, let me take your satchel to your donkey for you." Miryam (Mary) politely handed the satchel to

Yowceph as her sister Shalowmit (Salome) put her arm around her waist. Miryam looked into her eyes and Shalowmit began to weep and blubbered, "I will miss you big sis. Tell auntie I miss her and you hurry home." Then cook gently guided Shalowmit (Salome) to the side as Matityahu ben Levi stepped forward to embrace her. "Don't you worry about a thing my dear. We will keep a close eye on that husband of yours until you get back. That special day of yours is not that far away," said her grandfather, trying to be encouraging. Miryam kissed him on his bearded cheek and replied, "Oh, he is in good hands I'm sure. Please work on Miss Nanny Goat's attitude while I am gone will you." At that they both let out a little chuckle and she mounted her donkey.

They all waved good-by and exclaimed *shalom* as the small caravan began to go through the dusty street of the town of Nazareth. She glanced up at the neighbor's house across the street and noticed her engaged husband working on a piece of furniture but he refused to look up. She thought, *"What does Yowceph know!"*

The journey was long, bumpy and dusty but the small caravan traveled with haste to the tiny town in the hill country of Yhuwdah (Judah). Even the donkeys seem to understand the haste of their masters as they needed very little prompting as they ascended up the rocky trails of the hill country. Conversation did not exist except an occasional word of encouragement to the donkeys by the guards which gave ample time for Miryam (Mary) to contemplate the situation. However, her heart was at peace and at each step of her donkey the excitement grew in her bosom to share in the miracle of her aunt and herself as announced by the messenger angel Gabri'Yah (Gabriel) yesterday in the goat shed.

As they entered the edge of the small hill country town, Miryam (Mary) knew that her aunt and uncle were not expecting her because

Elysheba was not trotting down the dusty road waving her arms and jumping up and down with her Uncle Zkaryah (Zechariah) slowly plodding along behind her at a distance. Therefore, for the first time in her life as long as she could remember, Miryam made a peaceful and unannounced entrance into this small hillside community. They dismounted their donkeys and one of the body guards knocked on the brown ruff wooden door with his knuckles. The sun was beginning to set in the west with its usual beautiful canvas of multi-colors in the pre-dusk sky. The rap, rap, rap sound of knuckles on wood seemed to disturb the serenity of the moment prompting a stirring motion sound that could be heard from behind the closed weathered brown wooden door.

When Uncle Zkaryah (Zechariah) slowly opened the aged door to the surprise of Miryam and the body guards his mouth dropped open and he began frantically stomping his feet, clapping his hands and waving his arms like a frightened wounded bird. This spectacle sight was only interrupted by the trotting sound of the feet of Elysheba (Elizabeth) and her exclaiming, "Oh my….oh my, I just don't believe my eyes. Are they playing tricks on this old woman? Look Zkaryah its Miryam!" Zkaryah stood in the doorway with Miryam not saying a word but made gestures with his hands and shaking his head. Miryam kissed Zkaryah on his cheek and then greeted Elysheba with a hug noticing her rounded mid-section. Miryam kissed Elysheba on both cheeks and said, "*Shalom*, Aunt Elysheba."

As soon as Elysheba (Elizabeth) heard the greeting of Miryam (Mary) the unborn infant leaped in her womb as if skipping and Elysheba (Elizabeth) was filled with the Sacred Breath (Holy Spirit) and in a loud voice exclaimed to Miryam, "Blessed are you among women and blessed is the child you will bear! Why am I so favored, that the mother of my Master and Savior should come to me? As soon as the sound of your greeting reached my ears, the unborn infant in my womb skipped for joy. Supremely blest is the one who has faith and entrusts their spiritual well-being in the Messiah, because of the uttered words spoken to her from Yahuah that will be the completion of prophecy." In the meantime Zkaryah (Zechariah) motioned for the two body guards to bring the cargo inside and to warm up by the fire.

Then Miryam (Mary) burst out in a song with her beautiful clear soprano voice, "My vitality of breath extols in praise to Yahuah and my spirit jumps for joy in Yahuah, my Messiah because he has been mindful with favor upon the humble state of His servant. Lo! From now on all generations of age will pronounce and esteem me as favored because Yahuah has done great things to me. Pure and sacred is the authority and character of His Name. His merciful compassion extends to those who revere Him from generation of age to generation of age. He has performed mighty deeds with the strength of His arm and dissipated and routed the haughty proud in the minds of their heart of feelings and thoughts. He demolished rulers from their stately seats of power as potentates and elevated the humiliated. He filled up to satisfaction the famished with good things and He dismissed and sent away the wealthy empty. He helped in difficulty and distress Yisra'Yah (Israel), His servant, remembering divine compassion to be merciful, just as He talked to our fathers, to Abraham, and to his seed to the Messianic age."

When Miryam (Mary) had sung her last note, Elysheba (Elizabeth) was clearing the moisture of tears from her eyes. Uncle Zkaryah (Zechariah) was sniffling and dabbing at his eyes and even the body guards by the fire were overcome with emotion and extremely moved by the beautiful words of the song and the sweet melodious soprano voice of Miryam. Everyone stood motionless and speechless for a few moments as they basked in the beauty of worship to Yahuah. Eyes closed, arms raised and heads lifted towards the heavens glorifying father Yahuah. What peace, stifling serenity, breathless warmth and utter holiness as the Sacred Breath, Holy Spirit, filled the tiny house of *kohen,* priest, Zkaryah and Elysheba.

Then Elysheba (Elizabeth) quietly made her way to the kitchen stove and with the assistance of Miryam (Mary) began to prepare the evening meal and pack some food for the return of the body guards early next morning. As they were getting supper, the guards took the donkeys to the little shed out back and fed and watered them. They would sleep with the beasts of burden tonight so that they could get a very early start back home and not disturb the rest of the household in their departing. They returned to the house for the evening meal and when it came time for the blessing of thanksgiving for the meal it was then that Miryam realized that Zkaryah (Zechariah) had not spoken a word. Actually, he could not speak at all. As they all consumed the delicious morsels that the women had prepared Uncle Zkaryah (Zechariah) waved his arms making unknown motions while Aunt Elysheba (Elizabeth) interpreted in the famous Elysheba style of filling in all the gaps with colorful excitement and no loss of words. After the miraculous story and the explanation of Zkaryah (Zechariah) being a mute until the baby is born from the womb of Elysheba, the body guards excused themselves so that they could get some rest before the long journey ahead of them the next day. Zkaryah blessed and prayed silently over them for travel mercies from Yahuah. As Zkaryah showed them out the door, Miryam (Mary) cleared the evening meal table and took the dirty dishes to the kitchen area. Being fully exhausted from a long day of traveling and unexpected excitement, the three of them went to bed. Elysheba (Elizabeth) made a nice place by the fireplace for Miryam (Mary) and then departed to the bedroom with Zkaryah.

The next day Matityahu ben Levi went to pay a visit to his neighbor across the street to speak with Yowceph (Joseph) ben Ya'aqob (Jacob) about some very personal matters concerning his granddaughter, the engaged bride of Yowceph. As he closed the wooden door behind him he noticed that Yowceph (Joseph) was out front working on the piece of furniture that he was working on yesterday. Matityahu ben Levi noticed that his heart was beating against his chest a little faster and the palms of his hands were clammy with sweat. He took a deep breath and began walking with purpose towards Yowceph (Joseph). When Yowceph noticed Matityahu crossing the road, he gave Matityahu a nod of the head to acknowledge his coming. At that gesture, Matityahu ben Levi said, "Good and blessed morning young Yowceph. *Shalom.*" "And to you," replied Yowceph. Matityahu ben Levi continued to make small talk, "Young man that is a beautiful piece of furniture. So finely built. It looks like you are about done." Yowceph (Joseph) put down his piece of sandpaper and said, "Yes, sir. Just a couple more hours and I can deliver it to its new owner. They should make a good pair." At that they both chuckled a little and then Yowceph broke the ice, "I noticed that my future bride, Princess Miryam (Mary) rode out yesterday with a pair of body guards and did not return before evening set in. Did she return during the night?"

As Matityahu ben Levi cleared his throat, his tongue felt like three inches thick and stuck to the top of his mouth, "*Lo,* no...no she didn't. That is why I came over this morning because I need to have a conversation with you about that very thing." This puzzled Yowceph (Joseph) so he replied, "Is everything ok? How can I help?" Matityahu ben Levi looked all around and said, "Yowceph you might be some help. Can you come over to my house so that we can discuss this matter man-to-man without being the center of attention of the entire town of Nazareth?" Yowceph (Joseph) not realizing the seriousness of the matter joked, "What, you don't want to be the next subject of the long-nosed market women today?" However, when Matityahu did not smile or even acknowledge the joke, he knew something was wrong and instantly said, "*Ken,* yes, just give me a moment to brush off the sawdust from my garments and we will act like we are talking about furniture and then I will accompany you across the street. They might just think that we are discussing a wedding present of fine furniture from you to my new bride." Matityahu ben Levi agreed, "Fine, fine. Good idea." Then Matityahu ben Levi started making waving motions with his hands as if he was describing something noting the size of depth and width with his hands. Yowceph (Joseph) played along nodding his head one way or another. Then he threw up his hands in the air and pointed across the street to the house of Matityahu ben Levi. Matityahu nodded his head in agreement and they both walked across the street and into the house.

Matityahu ben Levi guided Yowceph to his office and shut the inside door and whispered, "This is a very delicate matter so I must implore you to speak in a whisper. I have sent cook with young Yowceph and Shalowmit (Salome) to the market and told cook under no circumstance to come home until the afternoon prayers have concluded." Matityahu looked at Yowceph for agreement and Yowceph whispered, "*Ken,* Yes, but I don't understand. What is going on?" Matityahu took a deep breath and in a soft voice warned, "You will fully understand when I am through the gravity of the nature of this conversation so I must sternly implore you that no matter what, this conversation stays within these walls and not even a breath or hint of our conversation must leave this room ever. Understand?" By now Yowceph was on pins and needles and whispered impatiently, "I agree and I swear upon my own life to you but I do not understand what you are talking about."

Matityahu began in a very low tone, "You see, the day before yesterday cook found Miryam (Mary) laying on the floor of the goat shed covered in straw and dust just before the sun had set. Miryam appeared to be dazed and did not have her wits about her. According to cook, she had not been acting right all day, just staring out the windows watching every move you made. Then before the evening meal cook sent Miryam to the shed to milk Miss Nanny Goat. However, after a long delay cook decided to check on Miryam and found Miss Nanny Goat running around loose eating her flowers. She caught the goat and took it back to the shed and that is when she discovered Miryam in her condition. You know how Miss Nanny Goat and Miryam don't get along so cook just figured that Miryam (Mary) had slipped in the struggle and hit her head."

With this information Yowceph got excited and leaned closer to Matityahu and said, "So that is why she left yesterday morning to see the physician in Yruwshalaim (Jerusalem)? Do you think it is really that serious or are you just taking precautions?" Matityahu ben Levi shook his head and motioned with his hand for Yowceph to keep his voice low. Then he said, "It's not that at all Yowceph (Joseph). Please let me finish without you interrupting me because you won't understand fully until the very end."

Matityahu continued with Yowceph now hanging onto every word that was being said, "I would have thought the same as cook if it had not been for the conversation between Miryam and myself just before she went to bed that night after the special *Chanukah*, Hanukkah services at the synagogue. I had just put the last log on the fire when Miryam sat down by my side and leaned on me. Then the story she told me was just unbelievable. She said that during the struggle with Miss Nanny Goat, she was visited by a messenger angel and he said she was going to become pregnant by the Sacred Breath of Yahuah and bear a son who will rule the nations to the Messianic Period. Then there was a big gust of wind that knocked her to the floor followed by a bright cloud surrounding her. That is when I cut her off because I could not take any more blasphemy. I informed her that if Rome or Herod heard of this they would kill her for treason. As you know the word from Yruwshalaim (Jerusalem) is that ol' King Herod is looking for any excuse to commit murder and the news of a new Hebrew King coming would set him off."

"However, she began to persist that she was pregnant and that even her aged Aunt Elysheba (Elizabeth) was six months pregnant. Therefore, I sent her to her Aunt Elysheba (Elizabeth) and Uncle Zkaryah (Zechariah) for three months so that maybe she can get her wits about her. However, my boy even though this is a wild and crazy story, you know that she is bright enough and quick witted to make up such a story to protect you." Yowceph (Joseph) was taken aback by surprise and interrupted Matityahu saying, "To protect me? Why and from what?" Matityahu cleared his throat again and his voice began to shake with nerves, "Now, now, we are both grown men here. If something has happened I respect you and your family and I will not require you to pay the required pre-wedding night penalties of fifty pieces of silver as required by Hebrew law. However, I must ask you man to man, did you violate the virginity of Miryam (Mary) in the goat shed?"

Yowceph (Joseph) was floored and felt like a tree in the forest had just fallen down on top of him. He could not breathe and felt faint. For what seemed like an eternity, thoughts ran through his mind. *"Surely he did not just say what I thought he said." "Are you serious, blaming me for her crazy story?" "Who does he think he is accusing me of* all people of violating his granddaughter?" "Doesn't he know me better than that?" Anger began to boil in the blood of Yowceph (Joseph) and when he had reached the boiling point in his silence he blew off the steam and said firmly, "*LO!* No! You know that I am more righteous than that. However, if she has been violated and if she is found being pregnant then I want the criminal brought to justice according to the law. Furthermore, if she is not pregnant and does not have her wits about her when she returns, then I want a private divorce settling this matter just between you and me. I love Miryam (Mary) too much to have harm come to her under any circumstances."

Matityahu quickly said, "Please! Please, lower your voice. We must consider the well being of Miryam (Mary) here. You do not want her committed as insane or stoned for possessing a demon do you? If a member of the Sanhedrin got wind of this they would stone her to death for sure for blasphemy if ol' King Herod did not get to her first! I am a business man and what you have proposed as a private divorce seems reasonable to me. I will return the amount of the dowry that you have paid so far and we will just keep this conversation between the two of us. Agreed?" Yowceph (Joseph) felt numb as if the world was spinning out of control. He heard his mouth speak but did not command it, "I agree." After giving each other one of their sandals Yowceph was led to the front door. As he walked towards his own house He heard Matityahu say, "Good luck on your new project and I hope I did not delay you too much in finishing that beautiful piece of furniture today." Yowceph did not turn around but acknowledged the farewell by lifting his arm and waving.

Shortly after the afternoon prayers, the body guards returned to Nazareth and stopped by the home of Matityahu ben Levi for the half payment of services rendered. They would get the other half after completing the return trip of the Princess from the hill country town back to Nazareth safely in three months. The guards dismounted their donkeys and walked to the front door. One of them knocked on the door with a bit of impatience since it had been a long day and they wanted nothing more than to get home before dark. Matityahu ben Levi began approaching the locked door saying, "Who is it?" One of the guards replied, "those who delivered the package that you had requested has been completed." Matityahu ben Levi unlocked the door and greeted the dust covered travelers. "Would you like a drink of wine or bread for nourishment?" he asked. Both guards shook their heads no so he invited them in to complete their initial transaction.

Matityahu ben Levi counted out the agreed amount of coins and inquired, "Did Zkaryah (Zechariah) and Elysheba (Elizabeth) look well?" One of the guards replied, "Oh yes, very much so. The miraculous surprise that they received really has brightened their lives and they appeared much younger than you had previously described. They were so full of vim and vigor with the news." Matityahu ben Levi assumed that he was referring to the surprise of Miryam (Mary) being sent to them and did not realize that they were speaking about the pregnancy of Aunt Elysheba (Elizabeth). Therefore he continued as he showed them back out the door, "Fine, fine that is great news. Now Miryam, did she seem content with the matter?" The other guard responded, "Extremely. In my opinion she was happier than they were about the matter but they were all so happy and rejoicing who could hardly tell?" Satisfied, Matityahu ben Levi concluded the conversation, "Thank you so much for your due diligence and the uplifting information you have given me. You have lifted a heavy burden off this old man's heart. I will see you both in three months. *Shalom* and may Yahuah continue to travel with you and keep you safe until we meet again."

As they departed Matityahu ben Levi could see cook and her two helpers making a direct line towards the house after a long day of shopping. They peppered him with questions but he told them that everything and everyone was just fine. He instructed cook to prepare a healthy meal to celebrate such a productive day at which she rolled her eyes and said, "*Oiy, vey* (Oh, pain) and men say that women are moody!"

3

The next three months seemed to just fly by at warp speed of a comet running across the night sky. Miryam (Mary) and the Aunt Elysheba (Elizabeth) were able to share so many 'firsts' together since they both were pregnant with their first child. Their bond grew from aunt-niece to friends to ultimately a mother-daughter relationship. Miryam (Mary) did not realize how much she had missed her mother as the orphanage in Yruwshalaim (Jerusalem) at the Temple dulled her senses of needing a mother. She had been so bitter that her mother had died and that they were raised in the Temple environment instead of the loving arms of a caring mother. Now being with her mother's sister brought her closer to her mother than she had ever been before. Aunt Elysheba (Elizabeth) did not try to replace her mother but instead taught her about who her mother really was. The time here in the hill country was too short and she was not ready to go back home even though she missed her family very much.

The example of Uncle Zkaryah (Zechariah) and Aunt Elysheba (Elizabeth) of how a marriage should work was invaluable. He doted over his loving wife and she was always there anticipating his every need as the perfect helpmate. Even though they were both aged, they still looked at each other with 'puppy love'. However, the foundation of their relationship was the deep devotion to Yahuah. Zkaryah (Zechariah) was not just a Temple priest in Yruwshalaim (Jerusalem) but he was *HaGadowl Kohen,* the high priest, of his household also. Their spiritual lives were rock solid and they both lived to bring

Yahuah glory with each action, every word, and all thoughts. Yahuah and the glory of His kingdom was the only mission for life no matter what the situation was. It was not the case that they were overzealous for Yahuah like 'religious fanatics' but that they lived their lives so that others could see Yahuah through them.

By now Zkaryah (Zechariah) was getting good at using body language to express his thoughts. Others in the village were also getting used to his gestures. On rare occasions his motions seemed more spastic than intentional. When this happened and there seemed to be confusion he would write out what he wanted in the dirt or on rare occasions used ink and paper but they were so expensive he did not use them much. Miryam (Mary) even came up with a good idea and had Elysheba (Elizabeth) sow the *Otiyot Yeshod*, alphabet, on a piece of cloth and he could point to the Hebrew letters to communicate with those who knew how to write. However, this was a slow process and not too many had the patience to spell out each letter when he could make a sign or draw a picture in the dirt instead. Even though he was silent as a mute, through his wild waving and stomping his voice had the effect of loud thunder leaving no doubt what he was trying to communicate. He definitely knew how to get his point across with the proper tone.

The last week of her three month visit, Miryam (Mary) helped Elysheba (Elizabeth) to fully clean the house and make sure that nothing with yeast in it remained inside because yeast represented sin. That meant that everything had to be removed from the house and the house was swept from top to bottom so that even a lonely dry crumb could not hide in a corner. This was in compliance of the Mosaic Law found in the book of *Elleh Shem* (Exodus) meaning 'these were the names', chapter 12:17-20, **"You shall observe** Chag HaMatstsah Lechem, **the Feast of Unleavened Bread, for on this very** *day I brought your hosts out of the land of Mitsrayim (Egypt); therefore you shall observe this day throughout your generations as a permanent ordinance. In the first month on the fourteenth day of the month at evening, you shall eat unleavened bread until the twenty-first day of the month at evening. Seven days there shall be no leaven found in your houses for whoever eats what is leavened that person shall be cut off from the congregation of Yisra'Yah (Israel) whether he is an alien or a native of the land. You shall not eat anything leavened in all your dwellings you shall eat unleavened bread."*

Before the *Shabbath*, day of rest, at the end of the week, the house had been put back in order spick and span and Miryam (Mary) was ready to head north to return home on the first day of the week. Zkaryah (Zechariah) also had a bag packed by Elysheba (Elizabeth) as he would be heading south at the same time towards Yruwshalaim (Jerusalem) to serve in the Temple. The day of departure came with the time commencing at the sound of beating knuckles on the ruff wooden door by two body guards that were to accompany Princess Miryam (Mary) back to the town of Nazareth. They all said their good-byes and the small caravan of Miryam (Mary) departed. Zkaryah (Zechariah) gave Elysheba (Elizabeth) a kiss and then mounted his donkey and proceeded in the opposite direction. Elysheba (Elizabeth) stood all alone in the road until both parties were out of sight. Then she received a hard kick in the belly from her unborn infant to remind her that she was not alone.

Yowceph (Joseph) was just beginning to pick up his tools for the evening, when he could see the small caravan of Miryam (Mary) and her two body guards approaching Nazareth. He removed his carpenter apron, brushed the sawdust from his hair and beard and then headed across the street to the house of Matityahu ben Levi. He stood at a distance from the front door as one of the body guards dismounted and knocked. Miryam (Mary) gave Yowceph (Joseph) a quick glance and Yowceph quickly looked at the other guard and said, "*Shalom.*" The guard responded, "And to you." Soon the door opened with Matityahu ben Levi standing in its opening and as he turned around he announced, "Come quick. Miryam (Mary) has come home!" First to make an appearance was her speedy Uncle Yowceph (Joseph) and then her sister Shalowmit (Salome) followed up by cook in the rear. Miryam (Mary) was helped down from her donkey by the body guard and she ran and greeted her family. As the family was exchanging their greetings, Matityahu ben Levi completed the business transaction with the body guards and they mounted up and headed down the road.

Matityahu ben Levi slapped Yowceph (Joseph) on the back and said, "Well, my boy she is home." The joyous greetings were soon brought to a close when now eleven year old uncle Yowceph (Joseph) gave Miryam (Mary) a hug and said, "Boy, you really have gotten fat." Miryam (Mary) in quick defense replied, "No, I am not! I'm......" At this Matityahu ben Levi quickly interrupted and said, "Cook, I always told you that old Elysheba (Elizabeth) could out cook you. Here is proof in the pudding. Now let's all get inside for supper." As he prompted everyone to get in the house he looked over his shoulder towards his neighbor Yowceph (Joseph) and said, "Thanks for coming. It looks like we will be finishing our conversation soon."

The shock of Miryam (Mary) actually being pregnant was just too much for Yowceph (Joseph) to comprehend. For three months he had convinced himself that Miryam (Mary) had simply hit her head on the shed dirt floor in the tussle with Miss Nanny Goat. Each day that passed he had embellished in anticipation her return making it closer to the day of the wedding. He definitely did not believe that wild story of a messenger angel and the unborn child being the New

King of the Hebrew people and other nations. Therefore, he began to carefully and scripturally consider his options according to the Holy Writ. Since, Yowceph (Joseph) was one of the town's leading *Towrah*, Torah (The first five books of the Bible written by Moses) scholars he knew that the Hebrew Law was clear. The only other thing clear at this moment was that he was still madly in love with her.

Thus he considered option number one. He could tell a lie, which is Satan's language and not Yahuah's, and claim the unborn child as his own. This would present three problems. First, he would be lying in front of Yahuah and would be a very unrighteous act. Second, the Law is clear in the book of *Dabar*, meaning 'Spoken Words (Deuteronomy), about pre-marital sex in chapter 22:29, **"Then the man who lay with her shall give to the girl's father fifty pieces of silver, and she shall become his wife because he has violated her and he can't divorce her all the days of his life."** However, during the private meeting with Matityahu ben Levi, they had agreed that if Yowceph had violated her and went through with the wedding then Matityahu would waive the fifty pieces of silver penalty. Again, this would be admitting to a lie and would disgrace Yahuah. The final problem with option number one would be with the unborn child itself. If it was a son, as Miryam (Mary) claimed then that son would be the firstborn to Yowceph (Joseph) and would be entitled to a double portion of his estate even though he was not from his loins. *'There is no way that I am going to give a double portion of my estate to a 'son' that isn't mine. That would not be fair to my real son that would be born later,"* thought Yowceph (Yowceph).

This brought the consideration of option number two. He could state the truth which was that he was not the one who violated her and clear his name and reputation publically. This would present three problems. First, it would bring shame upon the household of

Matityahu ben Levi and ruin his upright and important standing as the leading businessman in the town of Nazareth. It also would bring shame upon the family of Yowceph's own father since Yowceph (Joseph) and Miryam (Mary) were distant cousins. Second, and the most important Miryam (Mary) and the unborn child would be killed according to the Law found in the book of *Dabar* (Deuteronomy) chapter 22:20-21, **"But if this charge is true, that the girl was not found a virgin, then they shall bring out the girl to the doorway of her father's house and the men of the city shall stone her to death because she has committed an act of folly in Yisra'Yah (Israel) by playing the harlot whore in her father's house; thus you shall purge the evil from among you."** Cold chills ran down the spine of Yowceph (Joseph) thinking about Miryam (Mary) and the unborn child standing there being stoned to death. Once again there was no way that he would allow harm to come to Miryam (Mary). Besides, *"Why should that innocent unborn child give its life for the sins of his mother,'* thought Yowceph? Thirdly, he had made a contract agreement with Matityahu ben Levi that if she was pregnant upon her return, then Yowceph would give her a private divorce.

This ushered in the thoughts of consideration of option number three. It was the simplest and least complicated but it skirted the *Towrah Law* of the Holy Writ. He could get a private written certificate of divorce from Matityahu ben Levi and all his problems would be solved. However, once again this would present a problem for Miryam (Mary). She would have to be silently swept away to possibly one of her grandfather's remote and private estates to be put into seclusion to never see her family or appear in public the rest of her days. That would be like firmly holding a butterfly in the palm of your hand or holding tightly to a baby bird. The intention would be to keep them safe but in reality you would be suffocating and chocking the breath of life out of them. She would just wither away and die. Unfortunately, this is the option that he had willingly agreed to as a contract with her grandfather Matityahu ben Levi. To make it worse it was even Yowceph's idea!

Zkaryah (Zechariah) returned home to the hill country the day after meeting his requirements as *kohen*, priest, during the festival week of *Pecach*, Passover. Not only did he miss Elysheba (Elizabeth) but he wanted to be home before *Shabbath*, seventh day of rest (Friday sundown to Saturday sundown), which was also *Chag HaMatstsah Lechem,* the Feast of Unleavened Bread. During the third hour of the morning on *Shabbath* (9:00 a.m. Satuday), the first day of *Chag HaMatstsah Lechem,* the Feast of Unleavened Bread, Zkaryah (Zechariah) was in silent prayer basking in the fellowship with Yahuah when his prayers were interrupted by the voice of his wife Elysheba (Elizabeth). "Zkaryah, come here quickly I think it is time," requested Elysheba (Elizabeth).

He quickly ran to Elysheba (Elizabeth) and she said, "Hurry go get the midwife. My water just broke!" Zkaryah (Zechariah) bolted from the house and ran to get the midwife. He frantically knocked on her door and her husband answered. Zkaryah immediately made a rounding motion over his belly with both of his hands. The husband of the midwife said, "Dear, it is Zkaryah. I think you need to come here." The midwife came to the door and Zkaryah made the same motion again. The midwife responded, "*Ken, ken*, yes, yes, Zkaryah don't get so excited I still intend on being the midwife for Elysheba (Elizabeth) when it is time. All you have to do is come and get me." Zkaryah (Zechariah) became more frantic and made the same motion again but this time after the rounding motion he took both hands and hit his midsection indicating it being flat. The midwife said, "Stop worrying yourself to death old man, the delivery will go fine. You don't need to ask because you know that I have delivered all of the babies in this village and all safely." This response made Zkaryah shake his head back and forth wildly and then threw his hands into the air. Then he saw a clay pot near her flowerbed with water in it. He picked it up and threw it down between his legs. The midwife exclaimed, "What the.....have you lost your mind?" Then Zkaryah made the round motion over his belly, flattening it and then pointing to the broken water pot and the puddle of water between his legs. At this she exclaimed, "Oh my, her water has broken. Why didn't you say so?" Then she took off like a shot of lightning running towards the house of Zkaryah (Zechariah) and Elysheba (Elizabeth).

Being a senior *kohen*, priest, he knew not to reenter his house until after the delivery. Midwives and nervous husbands were never a good mix and the midwives always won out. Therefore, he waited for the husband of the midwife to gather some things that his wife would need for the delivery and Zkaryah helped him carry them to the house. They gave them to the midwife and after a gentle kiss by Zkaryah on the forehead of Elysheba the midwife made a shooing motion with her hands and chased them out of the house. What seemed an eternity of time and many miles of pacing back and forth on the front lawn by Zkaryah and loud moaning and piercing screams from Elysheba (Elizabeth) finally the moment arrived. The waiting, pacing and moaning were replaced by a loud wail that could spilt mountains from an infant. A smile with gaps in his yellowing teeth beamed from ear to ear accented by his gray beard. After the cord was cut, baby washed and skin salted, the midwife presented the new infant to Zkaryah (Zechariah) and said, "Congratulations, *ab*, father, it is a *ben*, son." Zkaryah held the precious bundle for a moment and then the midwife took the infant from him and returned it back to Elysheba (Elizabeth) for its first meal. Zkaryah (Zechariah) thought,

"*How fitting for this old kohen to have his only son be born on the first day of Unleavened Bread, the first day of the repentance celebration."*

The seven days of *Chag HaMatstsah Lechem*, the Feast of Unleavened Bread, passed quickly with all attention being paid to the newborn son in the house of Zkaryah (Zechariah). Many of the people in the community of this little hill country village and neighbors were filled with gladness and stopped by the house to share their joy with that of *Kohen* Zkaryah (Zechariah) and his wife Elysheba (Elizabeth). The day following the seven day long observance of unleavened bread symbolized the fulfilling of the covenant contract of repentance. In the case of *Kohen* Zkaryah (Zechariah) it was also a personal celebration. It was the infant son's eight day, the covenant of circumcision. The day was extremely beautiful as the dawning light seemed to have a little extra color in the horizon as the sun rose in the bright blue sky shining its warm rays upon the quiet hillside village. The invited guests and even some who weren't invited gathered outside in the front of the house while the husband of the midwife held the naked infant. As the *kohen*, priest, Zkaryah (Zechariah) would oversee the *brit milah*, covenant of circumcision and be the *mohel*, circumciser. He took the sharp flint stone and preformed the *muwlah*, circumcision.

That was the easy part but now came the hard part because he had to announce the name of his son but he could not speak. Since Zkaryah (Zechariah) could not speak some of the relatives standing in the front of the crowd started calling the infant Zkaryah (Zechariah) naming him after his father. Elysheba (Elizabeth) stepped from the front of the crowd and faced them and quieting them with the motion of her arms and said, "No indeed. In fact, he will be called Yowchanan, (John)!" Some in the crowd responded to her, "There is no one among your relatives who is called by this name!" Then they nodded at and communicated by gestures to his father what he wished to call him. Asking for a tablet to write on, Zkaryah (Zechariah) wrote in words, "Yowchanan (John) ben Zkaryah is his name!" The members of the crowd were dumbfounded and astonished.

Then all at once his mouth and tongue were opened up and he began speaking and praising Yahuah. Zkaryah (Zechariah) was filled with the Sacred Breath, Holy Spirit, and began prophesying as he held the naked infant above his head with both arms, "Adorable is Yahuah, the Master of Yisra'Yah (Israel) because He inspected and came to see to relieve His people and made a ransoming. He raised a horn of rescue and safety for us in the family of David, His servant. Just as He had uttered words through the mouth of His sacred inspired prophets from past ages. He provided rescue and safety from out of our hating and hostile adversary Satan and out of the hand of all the ones hating and detesting us. He showed mercy of divine compassion towards our fathers and to recollect His sacred contract. The sacred contract He swore to our father Abraham to give to us fearlessly out of the hand of our adversary Satan allowing us to be rescued to minister in religious homage to Yahuah in piety and justification before Him all the days of our lives." Then he brought the child down and held him out front to face him and then he continued, "You child, will be called an inspired prophet of Yahuah and will proceed as a herald in front of the face of Yahuah to prepare His road to give a knowledge of rescue and safety to His people by freedom and pardon of sins. Through the pity and sympathy of active divine compassion of Yahuah to us, in which He will come to see us as the Rising Light of Dawn from the east of the elevated sky to become visible and shine upon those sitting down in the obscure darkness and in the shadow of the darkness of the error of death, to direct our feet onto the Road of Peace."

Just before dusk, in the town of Babel (Babylon-modern Iraq) the five Magi and their apprentices met once again for night-watching as they had done together each night over the past five months. Mag Hammurabi instructed the scribe as follows, "Today it is Sivin (May) 19, 4 B.C. Present at the night-watching are; Chief Magi Hammurabi from Babel with his apprentice Marduk, Mag Nbuwzaradan from Opis with his apprentice Shadrak, Mag Kadashman from Sippar with his apprentice Meyshak, Mag Belsha'tstsar from Nippur with his apprentice Abed Ngow and Mag Zabaia from Erech with his apprentice Gungunam. The stars have all been on their normal paths of travel and no major conjunctions have taken place since the last light show five months ago. Tonight we have once again gathered to night-watch for any unusual star movement."

Then Mag Kadashman spoke up, "Magi brothers, earlier this week *Shabbethay the restful* (Saturn) moved into the hind legs of *Ariy* (Leo Lion) as if the first Adam was taking a servant position of the New King *Tsadaq the Righteous* (Jupiter)." Mag Zabaia added, "Yes, Mag Kadashman but notice tonight that *Shemesh* (Sun) and *Yareach* (Moon) have moved to the belly of *Ariy* (Leo Lion) above the *Regaleo* (Regulus) star as if they are standing guard over the scepter of Yhuwdah (Judah)." Mag Nbuwzaradan from Opis observed, "Magi brothers also note that *Tzadaq the Righteous* (Jupiter) is still with *Nogah* (Venus) in the constellation of *Bethuwlah the Virgin* (Virgo)." Then Mag Belsha'tstsar noted, "Look! *Tsayar the Messenger* (Mercury) is leaving *Sarton the Holder* (Cancer Crab) and is headed towards *Ariy* (Leo Lion)."

Mag Hammurabi began to be excited and exclaimed, "Magi keep an eye on those stars. Scribe be sure you are recording our comments and you apprentices keep watch and learn from your masters." Little Marduk then chirped in with his seven year old voice, "Magi did you notice that *Shabbethay the restful* (Saturn) the first Adam is quivering as if he is undecided on his next move?" Then in the blink of an eye *Tsayar the Messenger* (Mercury) made a dash to join *Shabbethay the restful* (Saturn) the first Adam in the hind legs of *Ariy* (Leo Lion). The messenger star (Mercury) positioned itself between the First Adam (Saturn) and the Sun and the Moon. This was interrupted by Magi Hammurabi and Kadashman as the Creator (Sun and Moon) gave a message (Mercury) to Man in the tribe of Yhuwdah (Judah). After a brief moment of conjunction with Saturn, the messenger star (Mercury) left the constellation of Leo the Lion.

That same night it had been two months since Yowceph (Joseph) had seen Miryam (Mary) at her return to Nazareth. She and her sister and cook did not come to synagogue anymore since her return. Yowceph (Joseph) and Matityahu ben Levi exchanged pleasantries but it was all a charade for those watching. After synagogue tonight Yowceph went straight up to bed. As he lay on his straw mattress located on his flat roof top, he stared at the twinkling stars dancing in the vast darkness. He thought, *'Tomorrow, I need to put an end to this charade. I can't live my life as a lie any longer. But what will my final decision be. Oh Yahuah please give me an answer so that I can be in Your will. Oh, what am I supposed to do....what am I to do......what am I to do...?"* Then Yowceph (Joseph) fell fast asleep with the cool night breeze blowing across his face.

Then a messenger angel of Yahuah brought tidings to Yowceph (Joseph) by the way of a dream and it was shown to him saying, "Yowceph son of David do not be frightened or alarmed to receive Miryam (Mary) to be intimate as your wife. For this reason, the unborn child in her has originated from the Sacred Breath (Holy Spirit) of Yahuah. She will produce a son and you will loudly announce His name, Yahusha meaning "Salvation of Yahuah" because He will deliver and protect His people from their sins. This all came into being in order that to finish and satisfy what was spoken by Yahuah through the inspired prophet Ysha'Yah (Isaiah) stating, 'The virgin maiden will hold in the matrix of her stomach and will produce a Son and they will call His name Immanuw'Yah (Immanuel) meaning 'Yahuah with us." After this, Yowceph (Joseph) woke up with two bright stars shining above his head. Then one seemed to disappear while the other glistened in the night sky.

4

The next day Yowceph (Joseph) went to the house across the street to his neighbor Matityahu ben Levi to explain the dream and to claim his bride. After knocking on the door he was met with an unusual, "Who is it and what do you want?" Yowceph (Joseph) tried to be discrete and said, "Yowceph your neighbor." The reply came back, "Who? I can't hear you!" Yowceph raised his voice and said, "Yowceph your neighbor requesting an audience with his father-in-law Matityahu ben Levi!" Then there was loud footsteps approaching and the door swung open with Matityahu ben Levi standing in the gap. He said, "Well, my boy I have been waiting for this day to come. Come in, come in." No one else could be seen or heard in the house. You could hear a pin drop. "Where is the rest of your family?" asked Yowceph (Joseph). Matityahu ben Levi replied, "When I was told that it was you by cook, I sent them all out back to the goat shed and instructed them all to stay there until I came and got them."

Matityahu ben Levi led Yowceph to his office and gestured for him to sit on the big cushion. Yowceph made himself comfortable and then he boldly began to make his case, "Sir, I apologize for not coming over any earlier but I just could not bear the news when I saw her. It just shattered my heart into a thousand pieces." Matityahu ben Levi nodded his head in agreement as Yowceph continued, "After feeling sorry for myself, which I have asked Yahuah for forgiveness, then I had to start putting all those tiny pieces back together in order for me to make a wise righteous decision pleasing to Yahuah. After

39

synagogue last night, I contemplated all my options according to the Scriptures of the Holy Writ especially the *Towrah* Law. Forgive, me sir but this also will seem a little strange. I went to sleep and a messenger angel appeared to me and instructed me to take Miryam (Mary) to be my wife at home because she will produce a Son and they will call his name Immanuw'Yah (Immanuel) meaning 'Yahuah with us' as prophesied by the inspired prophet Ysha'Yah (Isaiah). I am to name that Son 'Yahusha' meaning Salvation of Yahuah."

Matityahu ben Levi sat there on his cushion dumbfounded and in shock. Finally he got the strength to speak, "What you too? Why don't you two just tell the truth that you violated her in the goat shed that night since the evidence of her pregnancy now convicts you? I always considered you a righteous man but stooping so low as to lie about something as serious as this, even risking the life of my granddaughter? I should…." Yowceph interrupted Matityahu ben Levi and said, "I know that this is unbelievable but before you make any hasty decisions or say something that you shouldn't, I think that you should contact Zkaryah (Zechariah) and Elysheba (Elizabeth) and fully question the body guards of everything that they heard and saw." Matityahu ben Levi stroked his beard and said, "Well young man even though this is hard to believe, I do owe you and your family at least to investigate this last piece of the puzzle. You or Miryam (Mary) have never lied to me before until now so I will give you the benefit of the doubt until the investigation is over." Then Yowceph (Joseph) rose up from the floor cushion and said, "I will show myself out and then I am going home to start preparing a room for Miryam to come and stay with me in twenty-three days from now. That should give you plenty of time to gather all the evidence you need to see that the hand of Yahuah is in this matter!"

The great Vulture of Death was released from the dark lord

Satan. It slumbered with its giant blackish wings towards its favorite feeding ground where raw flesh was plentiful. A shadow of darkness fell over the great city of Yruwshalaim (Jerusalem). The palace of Herod the Great was once again in tumultuous uproar. He was so paranoid that he accused his father-in-law *Gadowl Kohen*, High Priest, Sadducee Rabbi Sethus ben Boethus, who was also called Yhowshuwa (Joshua) IV, of sedation against the throne. The charge of sedation came because two years ago the Pharisee's announced to Herod the Great that a New King would be coming to Yruwshalaim (Jerusalem) to rightfully claim the throne of David. King Herod the Great commissioned Sadducee Rabbi Sethus ben Boethus to study the scriptures and find out who this New King would be. It was now two years later and Sadducee Rabbi Sethus ben Boethus did not have any answers. Therefore, King Herod the Great had his fifty year old father-in-law the *Gadowl Kohen* boiled alive in oil for not disclosing the whereabouts of the coming New King.

King Herod the Great didn't trust either the Sadducee or Pharisee Sects of the *kohen*, priests. Therefore, he appointed Matthias ben Theophius to be the *Gadowl Kohen*, High Priest. This created a major problem in the Sanhedrin and essentially made King Herod's life more miserable. The two priestly sects united because of this selection for the *Gadowl Kohen*, High Priest. This move by Herod removed priestly governance from The House of Zadok which had been appointed by Ancient King David and had controlled the priestly governance for over one thousand consecutive years. The governance was given to a rogue priestly line from the last High Priest of Solomon's Temple Eniachin ben Seriah appointed by the King of Babel (Babylon-modern Iraq).

The next day following the appointment of Matthias ben Theophius as *Gadowl Kohen*, High Priest, he was summoned to appear in front of King Herod the Great. King Herod was in a very foul mood which was evident of the sound of objects clanking and thudding as they hit the floor of the throne room. These sudden burst of noise was then followed immediately by the clamoring of bewildered servants scrambling to get out of the way of these flying missiles being launched from the throne of the king. The two guards at the great golden doors of the throne room recognized Matthias ben Theophius and bowed their heads and opened the doors with caution.

Matthias ben Theophius could hardly believe the scene before his eyes as a multitude of servants were running here and there cleaning up the wreckage caused by the king. Strewn all over the floor were food stained golden platters with their original contents displaced in various heaps and patterns. The servants were also covered from head to toe with the contents of the food platters clinging and dripping from their clothing. Standing at the front was the king waving his scepter wildly, pointing with his free hand and screaming like a caged beast various insults and vulgarities towards those trying to appease him. Matthias ben Theophius stood there frozen at the back of the room not wanting to get in the middle of the nasty tirade or even get the debris on his sandals. Then all of a sudden the demonic eyes of King Herod met his in a flash and sent eerie chills up and down his spine that made him light headed and almost faint with horrific fear.

King Herod shouted, "Matthias ben Theophius, the great *Gadowl Kohen*, High Priest, of the Sanhedrin get up here and approach the throne! Do you think that you are too high and mighty to stand with your presence in front of me, the King?" Matthias ben Theophius tried to steady his self and began to proceed forward towards the throne as he replied in a quivering voice, "No your majesty. I was just in awe of your greatness." King Herod retorted, "Keep that lying tongue in your mouth! How dare you assume that you can spill forth your poison in the same air that I breathe without permission from my throne! I should have it cut out and thrown into the street as a treat for the dogs! Today I want you to go into the Most Sacred Place of the Temple with the incense censor from my throne so that Yahuah will know that it is I who is demanding His audience and not some lowly *kohen*, priest. Then you will demand for me from Him the answer that I have been seeking for the past two years. Where is the New King of Yisra'Yah (Israel) to come from? Is it from my royal house or from the House David, His pathetic ancient servant? Now get out of my eyesight and get to work before I change my mind of letting you live at this moment!" Then one of the servants handed Matthias ben Theophius the incense censor of the king and he departed walking backwards very quickly keeping his eyes upon the maniac king.

Matthias ben Theophius departed from the palace of Herod and went directly to Herod's Temple to bid his master's demands. He knew that he was not welcome among the other *kohen*, priests and received icy stares as he demanded the clothing of the *Gadowl Kohen*, High Priest. The Temple servants were the only ones who would comply with his requests with help to get dressed and prepare to enter into the Most Sacred Place to present the demands from the king to Yahuah. After getting dressed one of the servants attempted to hand Matthias ben Theophius the Sacred Incense Censor while another tied the rope around one of his ankles. The rope on the ankle was in case Yahuah rejected the presence of a *kohen*, priest and they were killed. Then the servants could just pull the dead body out without entering into the Most Sacred Place and risking that they themselves being killed by the glory of Yahuah. Matthias ben Theophius brushed aside the Sacred Incense Censor and pointed to the incense censor from King Herod. The few members of the Sanhedrin who bothered to show up looked at each other in amazement. Then with sly smiles gave a quick nod to each other in agreement. The House of Zadok would soon again become head of the priestly governance. Both Pharisee and Sadducee alike began to give words of encouragement to Matthias ben Theophius. As Matthias walked across the room towards the curtain that divided the Most Sacred Place the bells on the bottom of his robe jingled with sweet music. However, the other *kohen*, priests, knew that once behind the curtain the tinkling of the petite bells would quickly cease followed by a dull thud. Their confidence came from the book in the Holy Writ, 'elleh shem (Exodus) meaning 'these were the names' Chapter 30:9, **"You shall not offer any strange incense in front of the face of this altar."**

Matthias ben Theophius entered through the curtain into the Most Sacred Place and began to wave the incense censor back and forth creating a cloud of fragrance smoke between him and the Ark of the Covenant located between the outstretched wings of the two cherubs. Two steps forward and the tinkling music of the bells on the bottom of his robe grew silent followed by a slightly delayed dull thud. The temple servants quickly began to pull the dead body of Matthias ben Theophius from the Most Sacred Place. The Sanhedrin was convened within the hour of the death of Matthias ben Theophius and they elected Rabbi Yowzar ben Boethus the Sadducee brother of Rabbi Sethus ben Boethus, the ex-father-in-law of King Herod the Great. The Pharisee's were not completely satisfied with the election but at least they were appeased because the seat of the *Gadowl Kohen*, High Priest was once again in control of the House of Zadok.

A palace messenger quickly ran to the palace and informed the Master of Audiences of the King of the recent happenings at the

Temple. Upon hearing the recent news King Herod went into an uncontrolled tirade of how Yahuah was refusing to speak to the king and should be sentenced to death because of insurrection to his throne. This blasphemy sent the whole palace on edge fearing an earthquake, lightning or some other natural disaster to devour the royal palace at any second. However, King Herod the Great did not challenge the election by the Sanhedrin and never challenged the House of Zadok ever again. Yet, the Vulture of Death continued to glide and hover over the royal palace sending froth its dark clouds of putrid breath of disease from its enlarged nostrils. Daily the physical and mental condition of King Herod the Great deteriorated as he became more of a wild beast than that of a human king.

It had been twenty-three days since Yowceph (Joseph) the carpenter had visited Matityahu ben Levi about the situation of his granddaughter Miryam (Mary). Matityahu ben Levi had summoned and interrogated the two body guards on every detail that they saw and heard while taking and returning Miryam (Mary) from the hill country visit to her Uncle Zkaryah (Zechariah) and Aunt Elysheba (Elizabeth). Then Matityahu ben Levi traveled to the hill country and paid them an unexpected visit. After holding infant Yowchanan (John) in his arms he no longer could doubt the mysterious stories or that the hand of Yahuah was upon his granddaughter. Now it was June 12, 4 B.C. and he was in his study making the final arrangements with Yowceph (Joseph) to take Miryam (Mary) into his home as his wife. They decided it would be best to wait until dark and then Miryam (Mary) could cross the street to the house of Yowceph (Joseph) without the long-nosed windbags from the market prying into the private business affairs of these two families.

Yowceph (Joseph) held the hand of Miryam (Mary) tightly as they crossed the dirt street in the pitch black darkness of the night towards the house of Yowceph (Joseph). Once across the street he groped in the dark to find the door handle to quietly open the wooden door. He had left all the lantern's unlit so as not to shine any light on them as the door opened. Not a word was said between them and even their breathing was quiet so as not to make a sound to draw attention to themselves. However, on the inside their ears seemed to echo the pounding of their hearts against their chests with the excitement and mystery of the moment. Yowceph (Joseph) soon found the door handle and slightly opened the door and guided Miryam (Mary) inside. Then she stood to the side in the pitch black chiasm as a slight dull thud was heard when the wooden bar was slid into the metal groove to lock the front door. Then Yowceph whispered, "Stay right here where you are and don't move. I know my way around and I will get a lantern lit." Miryam (Mary) whispered back, "Ok. Don't worry about me because I am just fine. You did clean the place before you brought me here didn't you." Then she let out a very quiet giggle which brought a response from Yowceph (Joseph), "*Oiy vey*, oh pain, what have I got myself into?"

He soon returned with a lantern with the shadow of its flames dancing off the walls and ceiling. He handed the lantern to Miryam (Mary) and said, "Here come over here and sit down while I go and make a fire in the fireplace to get the chill off the air for you." Miryam noticed that Yowceph had already put the logs in the fireplace so all that he had to do was to get the kindling started on fire. Soon the kindling began to blaze and it engulfed the logs in red and orange flames as it emitted its warmth into the room. Then Yowceph went back across the room and stood in front of Miryam and took a hold of her free hand and said, "Welcome home Miryam (Mary)." Miryam looked up into his eyes and said, "Home. *Ken*, Yes my own home. Oh this is wonderful Yowceph."

Then she began to look around the room taking time to scan 'her home'. The room that they were in had slightly vaulted ceilings with beautiful etched carvings into the great wooden beams. From them hung fresh lavender that left a sweet and clean aroma that cascaded throughout the room. All the wooden furniture was exquisite in its workmanship of detailed curvatures and carvings. Multi-colored clay pottery accented the beautiful wooden furniture and was filled with various pampas grasses and dried flower bouquets with mixtures of small bright pink, yellow and blue flowers dotting larger flowers with a background of hues of deep reds, purples and oranges. This made the atmosphere fell cheerful, energetic and full of happiness.

Miryam (Mary) stood up from the elevated cushion and Yowceph (Joseph) lightly grabbed her shoulders and said, "Here let me remove your cloak for you." His touch was gentle but the strength in his hands could be felt as he removed the cloak from her shoulders. Miryam took two steps forward and commented, "Oh Yowceph this is so wonderful. How did you know to do all this?" Yowceph (Joseph) confessed, "Well, my mother decided that I needed a lot of helpful suggestions to turn this bachelor pad into a home for a young family. May I also add that she was not bashful in sharing her thoughts and rearranging things a 'woman's way' as she so firmly put it. Mother would just shake her head and say *oiy vey*, oh pain, this simply won't do!"

"Where did you get this floor rug? I have never seen this type of workmanship," inquired Miryam. Yowceph looked down at the rug with its tight weaving and its colors of browns, yellows and tans accented with pale blues and whites. The scene in the middle was a shepherd leading his flock of sheep through a valley of two mountain ranges with grey wolves lurking about the mountain clefts. Then Yowceph answered, "They traveled to the great city of Yruwshalaim

(Jerusalem) and purchased it from a small rug vender from Elam (Persia). Mom said that father and the souk vendor haggled for nearly two hours before they came to an agreement on the purchase price. According to mom, she thought that father got the best of him." They both laughed a little and Yowceph continued to give Miryam a tour of her new home.

The next room was the kitchen area where in the middle was a nice sized wooden work area with slotted holes filled with various wooden mixing spoons and spatulas. Under the table were neatly arranged shelves with ample storage room for various wooden mixing bowls, serving bowls, baking pans and a variety of different sized cups. Against the wall was a wooden cabinet with slide out shelves full of aromatic spices, various dried meats, shelled nuts, fresh fruit and sacks of flour and salt. The baking oven was just outside the back door with a pile of neatly stacked wood ready to use.

Then Yowceph (Joseph) took Miryam to her own room which was built off the kitchen area. A bright blue curtain served as the door with white fringe tassels lining its edges. It was tied back to the left side with a twisted golden-colored rope sash with three inch tassels hanging from the two ends of the rope sash. In the room was a dressing table and a plump straw mattress covered with white linen sheets and a warm quilted comforter with a flower design as the bedspread. The headboard had two folded praying hands on the top of each post and an open *Towrah* scroll in its center. Then Yowceph (Joseph) said, "It's late and I know that you have had a long day so I will leave you to your privacy." Miryam (Mary) blew a kiss to him and affectionately replied, "Thank you Yowceph. Thank you for everything, my husband." Yowceph got a lump in his throat and climbed up to his sleeping flat on the roof. He laid down on his mattress and stared up at the bright stars. Yowceph

(Joseph) did not have union with Miryam (Mary) until after she had given birth to a son.

That very night of June 12, 4 B.C. in the land of Babel (Babylon-modern Iraq) the Magi were faithfully gathered for their night-watching. Master Mag Hammurabi from Babel had all eyes watching the blinking lights in the vast canvas of darkness between each blinking light. As they were watching Mag Hammurabi instructed the apprentices, "In unison I want Shadrak, Meyshak, Abed Ngow, Gungunam and little Marduk to tell their Magi masters the current positions of the major stars." The five boys stood together and began, "*Shabbethay the Restful* (Saturn) the first man Adam has moved from the constellation of *Ariy* (Leo the Lion) representing Yhuwdah (Judah) and has moved into the constellation of *Sarton the Holder* (Cancer the Crab). *Shemesh* (Sun) and *Yareach* (Moon) have moved from the belly of the constellation of *Ariiy* (Leo the Lion) to the head of the constellation of *Bethuwlah the Virgin* (Virgo). *Tsadaq the Righteous* (Jupiter), the New King called the second Adam and *Nogah* (Venus) are still dwelling in the belly of the constellation of *Bethuwlah the Virgin*." After a brief moment of silence little Marduk quickly exclaimed, "The End" This brought giggles from the other apprentices and laughter from the Magi. Then Mag Nbuwzaradan from Opis said, "Look! *Nogah* (Venus) has more separation from *Tsadaq the Righteous* (Jupiter)." With excitement Mag Kadashman from Sippar said "She is going to leave the constellation to look for a new home." Then *Nogah* (Venus) disappeared into the vast darkness and could not be seen. Mag Belsha'tstsar from Nippur questioned, "Why would *Nogah* (Venus) try to hide and where is she headed?" Mag Zabaia from Erech replied, "This is very strange because *Nogah* (Venus) is always willing to shine her very bright light."

After three hours of intense watching the night sky, at the beginning of the second watch of the night (around 9:00 p.m.), Little Marduk burst out, "Look here she comes just below the tail of the constellation of *Sarton the Holder* (Cancer the Crab)." Master of the Magi Hammurabi jumped in, "Very good Marduk. She appears to be on the path towards the constellation of *Ariy* (Leo the Lion)." Then Mag Kadashman added, "She may be but keep an eye on *Shabbethay the Restful* (Saturn). He appears to be winking or beckoning her to stop at the constellation of *Sarton the Holder* (Cancer the Crab)." As *Nogah* (Venus) began to slow her pace Mag Nbuwzaradan muttered, "She is going to stop. She is going to stop and visit First Man Adam, *Shabbethay the Restful* (Saturn)." Mag Zabaia argued, "No way! Why would she leave the New King (Jupiter) and go into hiding with the First Adam, *Shabbethay the Restful* (Saturn)?" Yet *Nogah* (Venus) continued to slow its pace. Then Mag Hammurabi intervened, "You both have very valid points but remember Mag Zabaia *Tsadaq the Righteous* (Jupiter) the New King has not been crowned yet. As a matter of fact please note that *Regaleo* (Regulas) the ruling star in the constellation of *Ariy* (Leo the Lion) is all alone."

Then it happened. Another major conjunction of the planets took place in the year of 4 B.C. *Nogah* (Venus) joined *Shabbethay the Restful* (Saturn), the first Adam in the constellation of *Sarton the Holder* (Cancer the Crab). However, she settled a great distance from the first Adam and refused to come near him. Magi Master Hammurabi noted, "It appears Mag Nbuwzaradan was right. However, with the distance between these two stars in the constellation has a definite meaning. My wisdom tells me that the meaning of this major conjunction would be that with *Shemesh* (Sun), *Yareach* (Moon), and *Tsadaq the Righteous* (Jupiter) together in the constellation of *Bethuwlah the Virgin* that *Nogah* (Venus) is trying to tell us that an old era represented by the first Adam *Shabbethay the Restful* (Saturn) is about to come to an end and a new era represented by *Tsadaq the Righteous*, the New King of the Universe is about to be born because Sun and Moon are still abiding with him." The other four Magi concurred and they departed from the open viewing place to return to the home of Mag Hammurabi, their host.

5

The next morning Yowceph (Joseph) got out all his carpenter tools very quietly so as not to awaken the sleeping Miryam (Mary). Today he had to get that wooden shelf done for the spice maker. It wasn't just any shelf but it consisted of three upper open shelves for storage and the bottom two shelves were made into slide out bins to hold bulk spices consisting of four bins on each level. It was to be built completely out of oak except for the brass knobs on the slide out bins. He had the bottom two shelves done with the bins in them except for attaching the brass knobs, so today all he had to do was to be finished with the upper three shelves. He sat his first ruff cut oak board upon the two sawhorses and began to plane the surface smooth. The oak shavings curled into red tinted yellow spirals of timber spewing out of the mouth of the hand planer. The curled shavings clung to the hairs on the arms of Yowceph (Joseph) as he continued the back and forth motions. Soon the ground beneath his work was strewn with rapidly accumulating shavings.

Then he heard a stirring sound coming from inside the house. He put down his planer, brushed off his arms and carpenter's apron and began to head inside when Mosheh Klein's wife began to walk by in the dirt road in front of his house. He calmly put down his carpenter's apron, nodded in her direction and said, "*Shalom*. It is going to be a beautiful day today but it doesn't take long to work up a thirst." She smiled and said, "*Shalom. Ken*, yes. A fine day it is to be." Then the unthinkable happened. The biggest town gossip stopped walking and stood facing Yowceph as he was trying to reach for the door handle. He kept his wits about him and quickly engaged the conversation before she had time to pry. At least that was his intent of his thoughts thinking that it would be a good strategy to deploy. Therefore, he said, "How is Mosheh? I did not see him at the last Sabbath at synagogue." She replied, "Oh he is just fine, just fine. He just had a runny nose. He did not want to be a distraction to the other members of the synagogue with the sniffling and honking from his big crooked snout."

Yowceph forced a little giggle at which point she was quick to continue, "Speaking of synagogue…" Yowceph thought silently, *"Oiy vey, oh pain, here it comes right between my eyes.'* Even though the time had not reached mid-morning yet he began sweating profusely. The beads of sweat began running off his forehead and trickling onto his cheeks and beard. Then he heard the remainder of her comment, "I haven't seen the women folk of Matityahu ben Levi lately. Is everything ok with your neighbors across the street? I bet you miss seeing that petite bride-to-be of yours sitting up in the woman's balcony. I spoke with your mother the other day and she said that Miryam (Mary) was going to give you quite a surprise for your wedding night." Yowceph knew that this conversation had all the makings of a giant camel wreck and the ending was not going to be a pretty sight if he did not end this conversation and end it quickly. Therefore, Yowceph (Joseph) quickly added, "*Ken, ken,* Yes, yes, as a matter of fact she did. Only Yahuah Himself could outdo this surprise. It has been a pleasure visiting with you but I must go quench this parched throat of mine so I can get back to work. If I don't get that spice shelf done today for the spice maker you will not have cinnamon this week to make that scrumptious honey cake stuffed with creamy cheese of yours. Do you realize what an uproar

53

that would cause in this town?" They both laughed and she began to mosey on down the dusty street giving quick glances over her shoulder to see what the next move of Yowceph would be. He just politely waved and then proceeded to go into the house and calmly shut the wooden door behind him letting out a big sigh of relief.

Miryam (Mary) came popping from out of the kitchen area and said, "That was an interesting conversation to say the least. Your wit and humor are only outmatched by mine." The smile on the face of Miryam soon disappeared when Yowceph sternly replied, "Miryam, this is not a joking matter. This is very serious. If we are not very cautiously discreet, you, the baby, and even myself could lose our lives and cast a burden of shame upon our family names." Miryam softly apologized, "I am sorry, husband. You are right. I keep forgetting that this miracle is also a mystery that can only be revealed in due time. We have been given the privilege of being the caretakers of the fulfilling of the prophecy spoken of throughout the ages by the ancient prophets of old. We must never lose sight of the fact that this is not any ordinary child in my womb but the Son of the Most High, Yahuah." With that said, Yowceph (Joseph) held Miryam (Mary) in his bosom and gave her a kiss on the forehead. Then he said, "Have you had breakfast?" Miryam (Mary) replied, "*Lo*, no, and I am hungry. I was looking for something when I heard voices outside the front door." Yowceph held her chin in between the thumb and index finger of his right hand and said, "Here, sit down on this oversized floor cushion and I will get you something." He helped her sit down and then went into the kitchen area.

While she listened to the activity in the kitchen area as Yowceph was preparing her the first meal in her new home, she allowed her eyes to drift upwards to the slightly vaulted cathedral ceiling draped with fresh lavender that cascaded the sweet aroma throughout the house. The great wooden ruff hewn brown beams of cedar caught her attention. She could not see them very well in the light of the lantern last night and she was astonished at the scene before her eyes. Yowceph had made pictorial carvings into the great wooden beams of the major events of the *Towrah*. He began, with Adam, the first man in the Garden of Eden. It was a detailed scene of Adam, Eve and the serpent Satan next to a fruit tree with a great finger extending out from a cloud above them with streaks of lightning one on each side of the cloud stretching to the earth.

The next scene was the Great Flood with Noach (Noah). Giant waves seem to be pounding the huge three story box with pouring rain clouds above and various animals sticking their heads out of windows. This was followed by Abraham with a raised knife above his head as Yitschaq (Isaac) laid upon a stack of wood for a sacrifice. In that scene was also a giant hand coming out of a billowing cloud pointing a finger towards a briar bush with a ram caught in its midst. The next scene was Ya'aqob (Jacob) dreaming with a ladder extending to the vast heights of the clouds of heaven with figures going up and down the ladder. This was followed by a scene of young Yowceph (Joseph) being sold into slavery and taken to the country of Mitsrayim (Egypt) and his dreams of the seven stalks of corn and the seven head of cattle. The final scene on the first beam was Yowceph being second-in-command only to Pharaoh and the family of Yowceph being reunited in the land of Mitsrayim (Egypt) during the great famine.

The second great wooden beam began with the carvings of infant Mosheh (Moses) in an ark basket on the Nile River getting stuck in tall reeds and being found by the daughter of Pharaoh. The next scene that followed was Mosheh (Moses) standing in front of the burning bush. Then in great detail each of the ten plagues were displayed upon the rough cedar beam. The next scene was the crossing of the Red Sea with giant waves curling at the top as the Hebrew people crossed on dry land and the vast Mitsrayim (Egyptian) army of chariots and cavalry beginning to cross on the other side. Then the waves crashed down upon the pursuing Mitsrayim (Egyptian) army with chariots and horses being strewn and tossed about in the great waves of water. The scenes continued with the giving of the Ten Commandments written by the large finger of Yahuah extending down from a cloud and touching the gemstone tablets. The forty years of wandering in the desert for disobedience of not entering into the Promised Land was the next scene followed by a scene leading to the death of Mosheh (Moses) wandering all alone up the side of a mountain to die. The following scene was the crossing of the Yarden (Jordan) River with the twelve stones being piled up as a memento. Then came the scene of the Battle of Yriychow (Jericho) with the Hebrew army walking in circles around the great city. The scene continued with the blowing of the shofar ram horn trumpets and the great walls tumbling down. The final scene was the most touching of all. It depicted the young shepherd boy David tending to his sheep and carrying a little lamb in his bosom leading on a rocky road to a throne and being crowned king over the nation of Yisra'Yah (Israel). As her mind wandered back into the present, she found warm gentle tears flowing down her soft cheeks in total awe and humility of the beautiful workmanship that Yowceph had put into such a project of a labor of love towards his Heavenly Father. She thought, *"The Blessed Son of the Most High will get to see the living Towrah every day of His life."*

When her eyes slowly descended down from the vaulted ceiling, she saw standing patiently and quietly next to her was Yowceph (Joseph), her husband the wood artist. All she could say with a slightly quivering voice, *"How did you...I never knew. Oh Yowceph* the Towrah carvings are so beautiful and they are the story of the child that I am so blessed to carry in my womb." Yowceph then lowered an oblong tray of fresh dates, orange slices, small pieces of bread, baked eggs covered with a white cheese sauce and a small wooden cup full of fresh goat milk said, "Hush now. We can talk later when my work is complete. Right now you need to eat and be comfortable." He sat the tray of food next to her and continued, "I left some water in a bucket in the kitchen area so you can clean the dishes. I must finish the project outside and deliver it today then we can talk this evening. You must be careful not to make any sounds or be seen. I also sat a latrine pot by your bedroom door for you to use. I will empty it when I finish my work. You must stay inside for now so that no one knows that you are here until we can figure out a game plan. Tonight we will discuss what you will need to occupy your time and I will make arrangements to get it for you. Do you understand?" Miryam replied, "*Ken*, yes." Then she daintily began to devour the appetizing breakfast that her husband Yowceph (Joseph) had fixed for her.

Sixty days later to the East in Babel (Babylon-modern Iraq) on August 12, 4 B.C. while the Council of the Magi were sleeping their young apprentices were taking the last two watches of the night (Midnight to sunrise). Abed Ngow from Nippur and Shadrak from Opis were thumb wrestling and Gungunam from Erech was playing in the red glowing embers of the night campfire. Only Meyshak from Sippar and seven year old Marduk from Babel were watching the sky intently. *Shabbethay the Restful* (Saturn), the first Adam and *Nogah the Bright Star* (Venus) were still separated yet holding their positions in the constellation of *Sarton the Holder* (Cancer the Crab). *Shemesh* (Sun), *Yareach* (Moon), *Tsayar the Messenger* (Mercury) and *Tsadaq the Righteous* (Jupiter) the New King were still in the constellation of *Bethuwlah the Virgin* (Virgo).

Then it happened. Around the end of the first night watch (3:00 a.m.), *Tsadaq the Righteous* (Jupiter) the New King began to leave the constellation of *Bethuwlah the Virgin* (Virgo). Marduk and Meyshak looked at each other and then excitedly exclaimed, "Guys quit playing and go get the Magi. The heavens are on the move again." At that news, the three other boys jumped to their feet and ran as fast as they could with the older Gungunam leading the way. Not too much time had lapsed before Marduk and Meyshak could see a couple of torches parting the darkness of the night with eight shadowy figures heading up the path towards the night-watching campfire. When the eight joined them by the fire, the Magi directed Gungunam and Shadrak to extinguish the torches that they were carrying. Then the five Magi bent their necks back and looked up into the vast canvas of black dotted with sparkling dots of white light in the night sky.

Master Magi, Mag Hammurabi from Babel, spoke first as was the custom of The Order of The Magi to allow the Master Magi to pronounce his oracle of wisdom first before the rest of the order could speak. "Brother Magi, it appears that the New King is preparing to assume his new position. It is critical now that we watch with due diligence his every move from here on out." Mag Nbuwzaradan from Opis spoke, "Mag Kadashman, you are probably the most learned Magi among us on Hebrew history and prophesy. Do you think the New King is ready to assume the throne in Yhuwdah (Judah)?" Mag Kadashman from Sippar replied, "It is really hard to tell. My personal opinion is that the New King (Jupiter) will not assume the throne until he enters *Ariy* (Leo the Lion) and positions himself above the *Regaleo* (Regulus) star." The rest of the Magi concurred as they watched every finite movement of *Tsadaq the Righteous* (Jupiter) the New King.

Then one hour and twenty minutes before sunrise, *Tsadaq the*

Righteous (Jupiter) the New King joined next to *Nogah the Bright Star* (Venus) in the constellation of *Sarton the Holder* (Cancer the Crab). They were so close together that they became a single very bright light. It was so bright that *Shabbethay the Restful* (Saturn) the first Adam could not be seen. This bright morning star phenomenon lasted for about thirty minutes then faded. Then Mag Belsha'tstsar from Nippur noted, "Look! *Shabbethay the Restful* (Saturn) has disappeared and *Nogah the Bright Star* is leaving the constellation of *Sarton the Holder* (Cancer the Crab) and is headed to the constellation of *Ariy* (Leo the Lion) Yhuwdah (Judah)." Mag Zabaia from Erech added, "Also, note that *Tsayar the Messenger* (Mercury) has left the constellation of *Bethuwlah the Virgin* (Virgo).

Then little seven year old Marduk quietly spoke up, "Excuse me Magi. Master Hammurabi may I speak?" Mag Hammurabi looked at the other four Magi and they nodded so he said, "Go ahead young apprentice Marduk you may ask us a question." Marduk became excited and said, "No, I don't have a question but I wanted to say that you have sent me to Mag Kadashman to become a good student of the Hebrew people's history and prophecy. I really do pay attention even though sometimes it doesn't look like it and he scolds me to pay attention. Then he tells you that I will never be a good scholar. Well, I do remember something from his classes along with what you have taught me as my master and I think it applies to the morning star that we just witnessed. I remember the prophet Ysha'Yah (Isaiah) in chapter 60:1-3 ***"Arise and be luminous because your illumination has come and the splendor of Yahuah has risen on you. Because lo, the darkness will cover the firm earth and gloom of a lowering sky of peoples. But on you will rise Yahuah and His splendor on you will be seen. Nations will walk to your illumination and kings to the brilliancy of your rising of light."***

Little Marduk continued, "Also, the great revered Hebrew King David recorded his last words in the book of 2 Shmu'Yah (Samuel) chapter 23:2-4, *"The Breath (Spirit) of Yahuah has spoken an arrangement of words by me and His word of the discourse is on my tongue. Yahuah of Yisra'Yah (Israel) spoke this arrangement of words to me, He said, 'the Building Stone of Yisra'Yah (Israel). He rules over red fleshed human beings with justice (Tsadaq) and who rules in reverence of Yahuah, is as the illumination of the morning at dawn the break of day, the brilliant sun shoots forth brilliant beams of light makes a morning star at dawn the break of day not with enveloping dark clouds. Through its brilliancy after a rain sprouts tender grass from the firm earth."* The Magi stood there frozen in amazement and then the master of apprentice Marduk, Mag Hammurabi slapped Mag Kadashman on the back and said, "Yes, yes, little Marduk. I see that you do pay attention in class. What do you think about his recollection of your teaching Mag Kadashman?" Mag Kadashman replied, "I think the boy has a very valid point of what we have just witnessed in the early morning sky. It ties in very well with Hebrew historical record and Hebrew prophesy." Mag Hammurabi concluded, "It is settled then. The New King, *Tsadaq the Righteous* (Jupiter) is about to begin his reign. As soon as he moves into the constellation of *Ariy* (Leo the Lion) and settles above *Regaleo* (Regulus) he will have assumed the throne as the New King of the Universe replacing the old king, the first Adam." Then the ten night-watchers returned to the home of Mag Hammurabi and the sleepy apprentices went to bed as the Magi attended to their daily charting of the stars and planets and the study of their past movements.

That very same day to the West in the little village of Nazareth, Yowceph (Joseph) said to Miryam (Mary), "I think I finally have a solution to you having to live in seclusion and yet would satisfy the town gossips at the market square. However, I need the approval of your grandfather so I will go get him and bring him here to share my plan with you two." Miryam (Mary) questioned, "What not even a hint for me?" Yowceph answered, "No not even a hint for my blossoming wife." Then she stuck out her lower lip as if to pout and he smiled and quickly trotted out the front door. As he trotted out the door in the early morning light he could see the market square to the south just beginning to wake up as venders were starting to put out their wares and merchandise. Before he knew it, he was standing at the front door of Matityahu ben Levi, the mining Baron. As he knocked on the wooden door he recognized the familiar voice of cook croaking, "Who is it and what do you want?" Yowceph retorted, "I am the boogey man here to bring you misery until you open this door." Then there was the noise of quick shuffling of feet and low murmuring coming from inside the door and finally heavier footsteps making their way to the door. Soon the door bolt clicked and the door creaked on its hinges as the heavy wooden door opened just a sliver. Yowceph quickly said, "Oh come on Matityahu hurry up and let me in before the town wonders why I am standing on the doorstep of my father-in-law." Then the door opened and Yowceph was quickly ushered inside. The door was quickly shut and bolted behind him.

Matityahu ben Levi questioned, "What brings you here at this early hour of the morning young Yowceph? Is everything ok?" Yowceph (Joseph) answered, "*Ken, ken,* Yes yes, just fine. I think I have a solution to our little dilemma and it will finally give our families freedom from the chains of mystery and living a life of intrigue." "Well, I am all ears. Let me hear it," replied Matityahu ben Levi. Yowceph said, "I need you to come over to my house so I can share the idea with you and Miryam at the same time. She doesn't know anything yet and is on pins and needles until she finds out. Have young Uncle Yowceph bring over that broken chair of yours with you and it will appear as if I am fixing a chair for you." Puzzled Matityahu ben Levi said, "What broken chair are you talking about? I don't have a broken chair." Then with a swift kick of the sandaled foot of Yowceph, he broke the support spindle of a chair nearby. "Now you do!" said Yowceph as he was quickly retreating towards the front door leaving a bewildered and shocked Matityahu ben Levi standing all alone with the broken chair.

Within the hour as Yowceph (Joseph) was cleaning up some of the carpenter mess in the front of the house, the front door opened across the street and appearing was Matityahu ben Levi followed by young Uncle Yowceph carrying the broken chair. Yowceph called out to them so that any onlookers could get their ears full, "Ah, master Matityahu ben Levi and young Yowceph. I see you are bringing me that broken chair that I came over earlier this morning to look at. Let's take it inside where my spindles are and I will have you fixed up in no time." Then he opened the front door and guided both of them inside with the broken chair. The mouth of Miryam (Mary) dropped open as she ran and gave her grandfather a big hug and then ruffled the hair of her uncle Yowceph. After the cordial greetings Miryam (Mary) asked, "Grandfather, how did you break your favorite chair?" As the eyes of Matityahu ben Levi darted like guided missiles glared at Yowceph (Joseph), Yowceph began to become flushed with guilt of embarrassment. Matityahu ben Levi quickly quipped, "That is a very good question my dear. I am hoping your husband Yowceph can shed some light on this very subject!"

Then Yowceph the carpenter took the chair from young Uncle Yowceph and began repairing it as he began his discourse, "As I was praying to Yahuah last night asking Him for a solution to our problem, He gave me this notion that I know will work. As I must regretfully bring up pain from the past, you all know the unfortunate history of how King Herod the Great has murdered by assassination the family of Miryam (Mary). First her *Kohen*, priestly, grandfather on her mother's side and then Miryam's own father, your son Matityahu ben Levi. With this past history in consideration and the current mental state of the king according to the rumors from Yruwshalaim (Jerusalem) we could not risk the public knowledge of the secret and very private family wedding that took place several months ago at your residence Matityahu ben Levi. I would like to publically explain this very situation at synagogue tonight. However, Matityahu and Uncle Yowceph you must play along and not show one remote bit of evidence of doubt to the story."

Matityahu ben Levi being surprised questioned, "What wedding? First you break my favorite chair to share this puzzle with me and now you are talking about a wedding that never took place? I don't understand!" Then Miryam (Mary) chimed in, "Oh that is brilliant Yowceph. *Halal Yah!* Celebrate to Yahuah! Don't you see grandfather? Yahuah Himself ordained our marriage the night that I was overcome by the Sacred Breath (Holy Spirit) and began carrying His Son. Due to our family history with the palace of Herod it had to be keep a secret for the protection of our families and even all the residents of this village of Nazareth. The news of a jubilant celebration in this community could very well bring the untold wrath of Herod upon this quiet village!" Matityahu ben Levi began stroking his long beard and finally said, "Brilliant. Brilliant like a bright morning star at dawn the break of day! Don't worry young Yowceph and I will do our part tonight. Right son?" Young Uncle Yowceph nodded in agreement and the parties said their good-bye's and left to their own home across the street with a repaired chair as their mysterious cover.

When synagogue was over that night, Yowceph (Joseph) slipped to the front of the assembly and raised both of his arms high and yelled, "*Damam! Damam!* Silence! Silence!" The ruler of the synagogue said, "*Ken,* Yes, Yowceph do you have something to share tonight?" Yowceph continued, "Please all have a seat. I have something very important to share with you tonight that involves the safety of your families." The room was immediately quiet and all sat down with what seemed like a thousand eyes staring right at him. With nerves of steel and the confidence of the Sacred Breath (Holy Spirit) Yowceph began his public discourse.

"We are a small village where neighbor watches after neighbor and we lend each other a hand in time of need. In reality we are not just neighbors but we are family. I am going to share information with you tonight as family and as a family we need to protect each other from possible grave danger and harm." The synagogue began to grow nervous with the possibility of danger lurking about. People began to squirm, looked at each other with puzzled looks and most sat on the edge of their seats. "You are all aware of the history between the Herod family in Yruwshalaim (Jerusalem) and my bride-to-be. How King Herod the Great assassinated the *Kohen,* priest, grandfather on her mother's side. Then the Butcher King killed her father causing her mother to die of immense grief leaving Miryam (Mary) and her sister Shalowmit (Salome) as orphans."

"With this history in mind, you are all also aware of a planned public wedding between us. However, in consideration of the past history and our concerns for the safety of this village we decided that it would be best not to bring undue attention to this village knowing the current mental state of Butcher King Herod. Thus several months ago, Miryam (Mary) and I had a private wedding at her grandfather's house. This prevented a possible rumor to the king that we were having a celebration to remove him from the throne. We apologize if it appeared as if we were deceiving you or hiding something but we are very concerned about the safety of this village from the wrath of King Herod. Matityahu ben Levi has had enough bloodshed in his family and does not need any more. That is why he moved to our quiet village in the first place. He and his family have been a good addition to our community and has helped each and every one of you in this room in one way or another. I believe that you need to show your gratitude and respect for this honorable man and not question our motives for a private wedding putting the needs of the safety of this village over our own desires for a large public celebration."

The congregation all began to mutter in agreement with Yowceph and became unified against the madness of King Herod the Great. Yowceph once again quieted the people and said, "Starting tomorrow you will once again be able to enjoy that smile of Miryam (Mary) as she will come out in public. This brings me to another announcement. As you all know several months ago, which was very shortly after our wedding night, she went to the hill country to help her Aunt Elysheba (Elizabeth). Well, I am proud to announce that the wedding night was successful before she left and we are a family of three!" This drew whistles, clapping and shouting from the crowd as they began to congratulate Yowceph of becoming a parent. Then young Uncle Yowceph screamed at the top of his lungs, "Hey what about me? I was the best groomsman ever!" This brought down the synagogue in energetic laughter. Hand shaking, back slapping and kisses on both cheeks in congratulatory greetings went on for an hour. The mood of the village of Nazareth was brightened under the evening moon as each resident felt as if they had something over the dreadful power of the Butcher King that would never be shared even unto his last putrid breath.

Back in the palace of Herod in the city of Yruwshalaim (Jerusalem), King Herod violently tossed and turned as the black evil demon minions of Satan tortured his sleep. The great black Vulture of Death let out an eerie screech as ashen green saliva drooled from its gaping mouth and coated the palace of Herod in its vulgar slime. Herod screamed in his sleep but no relief came. The royal servants would not come near him unless he was awake because of his putrid stench from the yellow pussy wounds with maggots crawling around inside. He had not bathed for months and his rotting flesh permeated his bedroom that was now his prison of relentless torment and torture. He had become a beast of a madman and not the reasoning of a monarch king. The great city of Yruwshalaim (Jerusalem) was in a chiasm of deep darkness looking, desperately searching and fervently praying to Yahuah for a bright morning star to rise at dawn to forever break this curse of darkness.

6

Twenty days later on August 31, 4 B.C. everything seemed to be just another day in the quiet town of Nazareth in Yhuwdah (Judah). There was the usual haggling going on at the market shops and the town gossips meeting for their daily feeding of the none-of-your-business news. Children were playing games with laughter and squeals of delight. Even the low tone of passer-by camels could be heard in the air. Song birds were singing their chorus of sweet songs and the fluttering of the wings of constantly moving turtledoves filled the ears with melodious music. Dogs were barking and the constant rhythm of the blacksmith beating on the anvil could be heard next to the market. Miryam (Mary) and Yowceph (Joseph) were visiting in the front yard of their house about starting a wooden cradle for the soon to be born baby who was kicking in her womb.

Then there was a thick cloud of dust coming from the south road towards the market square. It was moving rather rapidly and was obvious that a Roman cavalry was headed their way at a fast cantor. People at the town square began to scramble to their homes and the merchants were left with empty customers. Was this the warning that Yowceph had mentioned at the synagogue nearly a month ago? The men folk began to gather about the time the horses and their riders reached the main square. The red plumage on their helmets indicated that they were sent from Caesar himself. Had King Herod died and a new king was being proclaimed? Did the Butcher King get orders from Rome itself to seek out Yowceph and Miryam? A multitude of silent unanswered questions filled the air as the commander halted his squadron.

The commander began to unroll a parchment and herald a message, "To all the citizens of the great Roman Empire by direct order of your benevolent Emperor, *Kaisar Augoustos* (Caesar Augustus). Let it be known that each province of this great empire has been levied a tax and given to each governor to collect such taxes in order to finance the generosity of your Beloved Emperor. This shall be accomplished by each citizen of this great empire to register at an enrollment assessment at the said head-of-household's family origin. This first enrollment assessment has been given to your governor *Kurenios of Tsor* (Quirinius of Syria). Any such persons not complying with this order by the end of the year shall be imprisoned and sentenced to death for insurrection against the Roman Emperor himself. When you register and pay your family tax you shall be given a receipt as proof of your enrollment and compliance to this order. It need not be repeated that non-compliance to this decree shall be fatal. Only the aged and infirmed shall have the opportunity to register locally by reporting to the tax collectors. This decree is signed into law effective August 1, 4 B.C. in the month named to honor your Grand Emperor, *Kaisar Augoustos* (Caesar Augustus)." Then the commander threw the parchment down at the feet of the crowd and commanded the squadron to ride to the next community.

The parchment was picked up off the ground and given to Matityahu ben Levi since he was head of the town council. Matityahu ben Levi took the parchment, opened it up and reread its contents. By now all the citizens of Nazareth had gathered to hear what was going on. After the parchment was reread a huge murmur went through out the crowd. Some complained and others cursed the Romans. Therefore, before the resentment reached a crescendo of a roar, Matityahu ben Levi raised his arms and shouted, "*Damam! Damam!* Silence, Silence, I tell you!" When the crowd had quieted he continued, "You don't have to like the decree but your reaction to this news at this tone of pitch could be interpreted as a riot according to Roman Law. Now let's be sensible and not bring any more calamities down upon our heads." Most in the crowd nodded their heads or muttered something in agreement. Just as Matityahu ben Levi was to continue a voice from the middle of the crowd asked, "So, just what are we to do?"

Matityahu ben Levi responded, "The only thing you can do and that is comply with this decree. The only other choice is to not comply and you will be hanging naked from a Roman cross at their new year's celebration of *Saturnalia* in honor of their god Saturn. My suggestion is that you get this taken care of rather quickly before the fall winter rains and snow descends upon our territory. Therefore, all who are of the House of David and the environs in and around the great city of Yruwshalaim (Jerusalem), I would suggest that you take care of this business during *Chag HaCukkah* (Feast of Tabernacles) while you are there for the weeklong celebration anyway. I know that is what I and my family will be doing."

That very night to the East in the city of Babel (Babylon-modern Iraq) the Council of the Magi were getting settled in for their nightly watching. Master Mag Hammurabi called upon his young seven year old apprentice, "Little Marduk since you have become quite an accomplished scholar please share with us the positions of the planets as we begin this evening," Marduk jumped to his feet and replied, "Well, Master Hammurabi thank you for bestowing such an honor upon your humble servant." His speech was interrupted by a rock hitting him in the middle of the back thrown by apprentice Gungunam from Erech. "Hey, what did you do that for?" protested little Marduk. Master Hammurabi scolded, "Marduk please continue without the flowery narrative. Wisdom states that the pride of a man goes before his fall." Marduk gathered his confidence and continued, "*Shemesh* (Sun) and *Yareach* (Moon) are in the constellation of *Bethuwlah the Virgin* (Virgo). *Shabbethay the Restful* (Saturn) the first Adam has disappeared while *Tsadaq the Righteous* (Jupiter) the New King remains in the constellation of *Sartan the Holder* (Cancer the Crab). *Nogah the Bright* (Venus) is in the constellation of *Ariy* (Leo the Lion) Yhuwdah (Judah) and *Tsayar the Messenger* (Mercury) is on the move just below the constellation of *Sartan the Holder* (Cancer the Crab)."

Mag Hammurabi stated, "Very good Marduk please sit down." Then Mag Nbuwzaradan from Opis noted, "Look *Tsadaq the Righteous* (Jupiter) appears to be blinking at *Tsayar the Messenger* (Mercury) to stop." Mag Kadashman from Sippar said, "Yes, I see but it appears that *Tsayar the Messenger* (Mercury) is not interested and is going to bypass him. This would lead him to the next constellation of *Ariy* (Leo the Lion) Yhuwdah (Judah) where *Nogah the Bright* (Venus) has settled in the belly." Next Mag Belsha'tstsar from Nippur added, "Did you notice how jittery *Shemesh* (Sun) and *Yareach* (Moon) are in the constellation of *Bethuwlah the Virgin* (Virgo)? They may also be getting ready to move." They all began watching the sun and the moon when Mag Zabaia exclaimed upon seeing the fourth major conjunction of the year, "Brothers, *Tsayar the Messenger* (Mercury) has just entered the belly of the constellation of *Ariy* (Leo the Lion) Yhuwdah (Judah) and has settled next to *Nogah the Bright* (Venus). I wonder what the message is for her?" Master Magi Hammurabi was not distracted but intently kept watching the constellation of *Bethuwlah the Virgin* (Virgo). Then he shouted, "Brothers, look whatever the message was to *Nogah the Bright* (Venus) it has prompted *Shemesh* (Sun) and *Yareach*

(Moon) to leave the constellation of *Bethuwlah the Virgin* (Virgo) and once again begin to free orbit. I tell you they are about to crown the New King. However, we just do not know where for sure except Mag Kadashman believes it will be in the constellation of *Ariy* (Leo the Lion) Yhuwdah (Judah) when and if *Tsadaq the Righteous* (Jupiter) settles over *Regaleo* (Regulus)."

At that moment once again little seven year old Marduk spoke up, "Excuse me Master Hammurabi. May I make an observation?" Mag Hammurabi took in a deep breath and looked at the other Magi who nodded with inquisitive smiles and then he answered, "Go ahead little Marduk but no funny stuff. Just state your observations and leave it at that. We are not here for you to show off!" Marduk stood up and addressed the wise men, "Magi masters I am reminded of a Hebrew Script that Mag Kadashman once taught from Mal'akiy (Malachi) 3:20, **"Will rise for you revering My Name, the Sun of Righteousness and healing on His wings. You will go out and will act proudly like frisky calves of the stall."** I think that all of you are correct in your observations. The Hebrew Holy Writ said a New King would rise. That means will come to power. Therefore, *Tsadaq the Righteous* (Jupiter) must claim the staff of *Regaleo* (Regulus) in the constellation of *Ariy* (Leo the Lion) Yhuwdah (Judah). The Hebrew Script also mentioned *Shemesh* (Sun) the Father of Creation. But we all know that where *Shemesh* (Sun) goes that *Yareach* (Moon) must follow as this is His Spirit when He is not present. Therefore, *Tsayar the Messenger* (Mercury) already has the message in Yhuwdah (Judah) represented by the constellation of *Ariy* (Leo the Lion) and *Nogah the Bright* (Venus) is also there ready to shine forth the message. I believe that message is for the New King to come to the center of Yhuwdah (Judah), the great city of Yruwshalaim (Jerusalem)."

Once again the Magi were silent for a moment amazed at

the young apprentice's perception. However, Mag Hammurabi interjected, "That is a very good theory young Marduk and I applaud you for using your head. However, it is very important for you to remember that if you want to be a member of the Magi one day that you must comply with the number one rule. That rule is that under no circumstances do you use the stars to predict the future. We only record and then bear witness to those events that have been pre-told in the heavens. Do you understand little one?" Marduk replied, "Yes, Master Hammurabi. I will not make that mistake again. I really do want to be a Master of the Council one day just like you." Then Mag Hammurabi said, "Ok then. We will leave you fine apprentices to the night watch as we go get some sleep. See you in the morning."

Then the five Magi left the campfire of the night-watchers and headed back to the house of Mag Hammurabi. After a brief moment of silence as soon as the Magi were out of sight apprentice Meyshak from Sippar said, "Marduk. I don't care what your master said. I think you are right." Then the other three apprentices said, "Us too." Marduk never took his eyes off of the night sky and said, "Thanks guys but Master is right. We must never dishonor our craft by using the stars to predict the future. We must use it as a general warning of events to come but to add our own interjections would be entirely wrong!" Then Meyshak said, "I agree but I still think you are right!" Marduk replied, "Thanks Meyshak. You are a good friend."

To the West in the country of Yhuwdah (Judah) in the great city of Yruwshalaim (Jerusalem), all was a buzz from the announcement of the enrollment assessment. This city was already overflowing every year at this time because of the fall celebration of *Chag HaCukkah,* Feast of Tabernacles. The required Hebrew celebration was only two and a half weeks away and the merchants were just getting their souks ready for the giant influx of customers willing to purchase their wares. Now with the announcement coming directly from Rome itself the decree added extra pressure and preparation for this great city to be ready. Normally the city would quadruple for the eight day celebration, however with the required decree the city was expected to swell tenfold for possibly thirty days. The merchants weren't ready, the government wasn't ready and even the citizens were not ready to deal with the magnitude of this year's celebration.

With King Herod basically bedridden, his son Antipas took charge and decided that he would take a tour of the city to see what needed to be done in just over two weeks to handle the onslaught of visitors and the influx of professional criminals who would come to make easy pickings of overcrowded and naïve visitors. The Lower City in the Tyropoeon Valley could fend for itself or disappear for all he cared but he wanted to focus on the wealthy Upper City, the trading district of Bezetha and the Temple area. His plan was to first survey the wealthy Upper City, then move on to the Temple with the final inspection of the Bezetha District. He would employ his largest litter to carry himself plus two scribes commissioned to record his findings and also his thoughts on needed improvements. The large litter would be carried on the shoulders of a dozen *Cushite* (Ethiopian) eunuchs who wore pure white loin cloths adorned with gold braded belts of rope. The litter itself was draped in white Mitsrayim (Egyptian) linen with golden scallops accenting the fringes. The two curtains on each side were drawn and tied back so that he could have full vision of both sides of the streets. Above each side entrance was ostrich plumage fanning out towards the street as if to create a small amphitheater look. On the top of each of the four corner posts sat a twelve-inch golden elephant standing on its hind two legs with its trunk reaching high into the air as if to trumpet the forthcoming of the litter. Of course the entourage would not be complete without four mounted patrols and two-dozen armed palace guards to keep the paths cleared and provide protection.

As the litter passed by the Gennath Gate Antipas took note that he needed to triple security at the gate with fully battle ready guards and only those with special passes sent by invitation only could enter into the Upper City. Each household in the Upper City would be issued a rationed amount of passes to keep the Upper City from becoming too crowded. As they passed the Hasmonaean Palace of the Old Maccabim Dynasty, Antipas turned his head away because the Herod's hated the pious family of the Maccabim. Now the palace was used as the residence for the *Gadowl Kohen,* High Priest. Before the royal litter could reach the bridge that lead from the Hasmonaean Palace he noticed several members of the Sanhedrin walking from the Temple to the house of the High Priest. Sadducees and Pharisees were arguing vehemently. This distracted his mind from preparing the great city for the insurgence of visitors coming for the celebration and the enrollment assessment. He commanded the royal litter to come to a stop and shouted out the side window, "Hey, Pharisee. Come here!"

One of the Pharisees looked at the royal litter and Antipas waved for him to approach the litter. The Pharisee obliged and when he was near the litter he said, "Your Highness how may your servant serve you Sire?" Prince Antipas being short on time and patience quipped, "What is all the commotion from the Temple? Shouldn't the Sanhedrin be preparing for the *Chag HaCukkah,* Feast of Tabernacles?" The Pharisee grabbed both sides of his prayer shawl and said, "Sire, haven't you heard? *Gadowl Kohen,* High Priest, Rabbi Yowzar ben Boethus has become gravely ill and according to the Temple physician will not be able to perform at the Great Feast. Therefore, we have taken his seat away and given it to his brother

Rabbi Eleazar ben Boethus another 'pig-brained' Sadducee." At the mention of the word pig, the Pharisee spat upon the ground as was the Hebrew custom when something unclean was said showing complete contempt for what was uttered. Prince Antipas shook his hand crop out the window of the litter and said, "My father the king expects none of this religious squabbling and disharmony to exist during the festival this year. Do you understand? You give that message to the rest of the Sanhedrin. If one hint of disunion reaches the ears to the palace during this celebration I will personally be returning for your head to be separated by the sharp cold blade of my sword. Do I make myself very clear?" "*Ken*, Yes, Sire. I will deliver the message for His Majesty, your father," whined the Pharisee. Then Prince Antipas signaled for the royal entourage to cross the bridge towards the Temple area.

He had the scribes to make note that a squad of ten guards was to be placed at the entrance of the mouth of the bridge and only allow those to enter from the Royal Porch onto the bridge that leads to the Upper City to be members of the Sanhedrin or of the Royal Family. He decided to leave the security and the keeping of the peace in this area of the city to the Sanhedrin and the Temple Guards. He was sure that the Pharisee understood his final point of keeping the peace. As they exited the Temple Area through the Sheep Gate next to the Fortress of Antonia into the Bezetha District, once again the scribes were ordered to triple security at the Sheep Gate and to have around the clock armed archers stationed at the Fortress of Antonia in case the guards at the gate needed help. This aided the Temple Guards to keep control of the large crowds pouring into the Temple for worship.

Prince Antipas quickly noted that the Bezetha District would be hard to manage as the local merchants were already expanding into every possible space with their souks to display their wares and merchandise. If the great city of Yruwshalaim (Jerusalem) swelled to expectations then there would hardly be even room for a litter to be carried through the narrow streets of this district. The homes would be lined with wall to wall guests renting every square inch of floor space and even space on the flat roofs for sleeping accommodations of the massive crowd of visitors. He would have to coordinate with the governor to utilize one hundred mounted patrols day and night to keep the massive crowds under control and to keep the traffic on the crowded streets moving. It was very obvious that space would be very limited if non-existent, patience will be short-fused, tempers will be red hot, an abundance of intoxicating wine and hard liquor will flow freely, and every pleasure known to satisfy man will be readily available to meet the expected demands of the travelers.

The sun was beginning to set in the west as the royal entourage and litter returned to the Gennath Gate that leads to the Upper City. As the litter halted in front of the Palace of Herod, Prince Antipas could feel the gloom that seemed to hang over the palace. His father, the king, was not a healthy man and it would not take much to push him over the edge. As the eunuchs lowered the royal litter to the ground, all Prince Antipas could hope for his father, King Herod the Great during the festival this year as he climbed out of the litter was 'Peace on Earth' and 'Goodwill Towards Men'.

7

The day was fast approaching for those who were traveling to the great city of Yruwshalaim (Jerusalem) to ready themselves to leave to celebrate the seven day feast of *Chag HaCukkah,* Feast of Tabernacles. It was a four to four and a half day journey to the great city depending upon which route was taken. This was the very reason that Yowceph (Joseph) and Miryam (Mary) were headed across the street to the home of her grandfather Matityahu ben Levi to discuss the route to be taken by their family. As they were crossing the dusty street, they noticed Uncle *Qatan Yow,* 'Little Joe', as he was affectionately called now that Yowceph (Joseph) was a member of the family, sitting outside the front door. When they had reached the middle of the dusty street Miryam said, "*Shalom Qatan Yow,* Greetings Little Joe." He refused to look up and replied back, "*Shalom.*" Now they were standing in front of him and Yowceph (Joseph) remarked, "What's wrong *Qatan Yow,* Little Joe, have you been banned from the house?"

Eleven year old *Qatan Yow* (Little Joe), stuck out his pouting bottom lip and said, "*Ken,* yes, cook threw me out because she caught me sneaking some of her freshly made *haroset!*" Miryam (Mary) licked her lips and said, "*Oiy vey,* oh pain, *haroset*! No one can resist that mixture of fresh apples, almonds, fine sugarcane, cinnamon and grated lemon peels mixed in sweet red wine. What a delight to the tummy! Don't feel bad *Qatan Yow* (Little Joe) I couldn't resist that either. Come on show us inside." *Qatan Yow* (Little Joe) smiled as Yowceph (Joseph) ruffled his black curly head of hair and *Qatan Yow* jumped up, opened the door and shouted, "Everyone, Yowceph and Miryam are here!" Then the patter of feet could be heard coming from all directions of the house. First to arrive was thirteen year old Shalowmit (Salome) squealing with delight to see her older sister Miryam (Mary). Then came Matityahu ben Levi who gave Yowceph and Miryam a kiss on both cheeks to welcome them. Lastly came cook with a wooden spatula from the kitchen area exclaiming, "At last someone who knows how to cook!" as she shot an exasperating look at Shalowmit (Salome). "Oh cook, it is good to see you too. It can't be that bad can it?" as Miryam looked towards her younger sister. Cook began clicking her tongue and Shalowmit (Salome) defensively replied, "Hey, I at least try. Don't I?" Then grandfather, Matityahu ben Levi added, "Honestly, I think that we could sell the cooking of 'at least I try' results of Shalowmit to the Hebrew army as weapons of war against the Roman's. We could be an independent nation again in no time." At that they all burst out into rolling laughter with even Shalowmit (Salome) finding the comment a bit funny even though it was aimed at her pitiful excuse of fixing an edible meal.

When the laughter had died down, Matityahu ben Levi asked, "So what brings you two over here to visit this morning?" Then Yowceph (Joseph) answered, "Well, sir, Miryam and I are at a bit of a disagreement of which path to take. I want to go the easier and shorter route through *erets beniy gowlah*, land of the sons of captivity (Samaria) to make it easier upon Miryam and the baby. However, Miryam insists that no member of her family would ever be caught passing through *erets beniy gowlah*, land of the sons of captivity (Samaria) for any reason, especially for one of comfort and ease." Matityahu ben Levi interjected, "My boy, she is correct. Remember she is of royal descent. She must never be soiled by being near those forsaken people of the *beniy gowlah*, sons of captivity (Samaritans). I will provide a donkey for her to travel to insure her comfort." Miryam (Mary) protested, "I will walk thank you. I would be most uncomfortable sitting on a bouncing animal with my belly the size of a watermelon trying to be shoved up under my ribcage for ninety miles. You men just don't understand! Cook tell them!" Cook didn't say a word but she put both hands on her hips and shot the two men a look of steel daggers that cut to the very core of their souls while at the same time clucking her tongue.

Yowceph quickly replied in surrender, "Ok, it is settled then. Miryam will walk with the rest of us and we will go the long way." Matityahu ben Levi added, "*Qatan Yow* (Little Joe) and I must travel ahead of you on horses to be in Yruwshalaim (Jerusalem) a few days early before *Chag HaCukkah*, Feast of Tabernacles, to attend to some mining business with a few Roman officials. We will get the required passes from Ya'kov Melek'Beyth Aer (James Henry Ayers) the fan maker and his son Chizqiy (Charles) and meet you two at the Gennath Gate to the Upper City at sundown on the thirteenth of *Tishri* (September). That way you can enter into the Upper City to get settled before the *chag*, feast begins after sundown." Miryam (Mary) stated, "That is a good plan. It will be good to spend some time in the old neighborhood again. Sister, Shalowmit I wish you were going along also because I know you were too young to remember much of the old neighborhood in the Upper City." Shalowmit (Salome) quipped, "Oh no, sister, I need to stay here and perfect my unique cooking skills so I can catch a man like you." At that comment cook threw her arms into the air and spun on her heels and headed back to the kitchen area muttering under her breath, "*Oiy vey* (oh pain), *oiy vey* (oh pain), *oiy vey* (oh pain).....!" Shaking his head and chuckling, Yowceph (Joseph) said, "Very well. We will plan to leave a little earlier then so that we can travel directly to *Beyth Lechem* (Bethlehem) and get the business of registering for the family tax of the enrollment assessment over with so that Miryam does not have to fight the crowds during *Chag HaCukkah*, Feast of Tabernacles."

Matityahu ben Levi agreed, "That is a good plan. *Qatan Yow* (Little Joe) and I will already be registered that way none of us will have to leave the great city of Yruwshalaim (Jerusalem) once the *chag*, feast begins. We can all stay safe in the Upper City near the Temple until the celebration is over." They all shook their heads in agreement, said their good-byes and Yowceph (Joseph) and Miryam (Mary) returned to their own home across the street to begin the process of preparing for the trip. They would plan on leaving at sunrise of the ninth of *Tishri* (September) giving them an extra half a day to get registered for the tax in *Beyth Lechem* (Bethlehem), travel the five miles to Yruwshalaim (Jerusalem) and meet Matityahu ben Levi and *Qatan Yow* (Little Joe) at the Gennath Gate where accommodations in the Upper City would be waiting for them at the home of Ya'kov Melek'Beyth Aer (James Henry Ayers) the fan maker.

While Miryam was busy baking and packing food for the four and a half day journey, Yowceph was busy in the carpenter shop out back making a surprise of his own. He was going to fashion a portable stool for Miryam to sit on when they stopped to rest along the way. That way she did not have to get up and down from the ground. He found a good piece of lightweight cypress wood and cut out a round twelve inch diameter circle that was two inches thick. Then he began to bore three holes in the circle that would hold the pegs for the legs. Once that was completed he cut out three legs that were eighteen inches in length from cedar wood. This wood was still lightweight but yet more durable than cypress. He whittled the ends of the three legs so that the pegs would go securely into the peg holes of the circular seat.

Next he bored out two holes in each of the three legs where he would fit a horizontal brace connecting the three legs for support. Finally, he cut out three supports and whittled both ends of the supports until they fit snugly into the peg holes of the legs. The whole assemble only weighed about ten pounds and was tied securely together with a leather strap for the ease of carrying on his back during travel. It took him about two days to complete but when he was finished he just grinned from ear to ear. He would not show Miryam until the first rest stop during their travels to surprise her and the rest of the travelers. He thought, *"This might catch on and I get several orders while on the journey to keep me busy during the upcoming winter months. A little extra income never hurts especially during the winter season."*

On the afternoon of the eighth of *Tishri* (September) Miryam (Mary) went across the street to say good-by to her sister and cook while Yowceph (Joseph) was making the final arrangements with the old spice maker to watch the house and his carpenter's shop. Her grandfather Matityahu ben Levi and her eleven year old Uncle *Qatan Yow* (Little Joe) had left for Yruwshalaim (Jerusalem) three days earlier and would arrive in the great city tomorrow to register and to attend to mining business. Miryam knocked on the big wooden door and soon the patter of feet could be heard coming from the inside. Shalowmit (Salome) opened the door and cheerfully said, *"Shalom,* sister." Then she greeted Miryam with a kiss on both cheeks. Miryam (Mary) returned the greetings and they both proceeded to the kitchen area where cook was busy.

The three women sat down and chatted about the exciting travel back to the great city of Yruwshalaim (Jerusalem), the upcoming rainy season, the rumor of the insane condition of King Herod the Great, chitter-chatter female conversations that each of them had heard at the market square this week and even how the wife of

Mosheh Klein, the biggest town gossip was caught snooping into the affairs of the leader of the synagogue banning her for three moons from the synagogue like a leper. When Miryam looked up from the intense conversation she noticed that the light was beginning to dim outside so she excused herself and said her good-byes to head home across the street before sundown where Yowceph would be waiting for her. Just as Miryam was about to make her way to the front door, cook said, "Wait my dear. I made something for you to take on the trip with you." Then she handed Miryam a large container of *haroset* dessert and a cloth bag of thin sweet bread wafer crackers to use for dipping into the delectable dessert. "Oh cook you shouldn't have!" exclaimed Miryam (Mary). They gave each other a long hug and then Miryam went out the front door. Just as it was about to close Shalowmit (Salome) yelled, "May the hand of Yahuah become a hedge of thorns to protect your journey with safety and may it guide you safely back home again!" Miryam blew her a kiss and then waved good-by as the big wooden door closed shut with a dull thud sound.

When Miryam (Mary) had crossed the dusty street into her own home, she found her husband Yowceph (Joseph) waiting for her. As she closed the front door behind her Yowceph said, "Did you have a good time?" Miryam replied, "Oh yes and look cook made some *haroset* dessert for us to take on the trip." Yowceph pleaded, "Do we have to wait for the trip? Let's sample some of it right now!" Then Miryam scolded, "You are as bad as *Qatan Yow* (Little Joe)! If cook was here she would send you straight to bed without supper!" Then Yowceph tickled her sides and teased, "Oh but she is not here and you are also drooling for just a little sample of a taste." Miryam answered, "Ok, I surrender! Stop tickling me before I drop it on the floor. I will bring out a small platter and we can eat it while supper is cooking. But mind you a very small platter so this can last the whole trip."

Then she went into the kitchen area to begin a hearty supper for the long journey tomorrow. After their treat of *haroset* they ate a hearty meal of roasted lamb, fresh fruit and a mixture of boiled vegetables of carrots, onions, garlic, and broccoli. They both retired to their respective bedrooms early that evening to be fully rested the next morning as they began the long four and a half day journey of ninety miles to Yruwshalaim. Yowceph (Joseph) quickly dozed off to sleep as the stars playfully danced above him in the night sky.

That same evening to the Far East in the city of Babel (Babylon- modern Iraq) the night watchers had gathered for their nightly observation. Master Magi Hammurabi from Babel began the evening watch as was his custom, "Brother Magi, the current position of the stars is as follows: *Nogah the Bright* (Venus) and *Tsayar the Messenger* (Mercury) are in the belly of the constellation *Ariy* (Leo the Lion) Yhuwdah (Judah). *Tsadaq the Righteous* (Jupiter) New King is content to be in the constellation of *Sarton the Holder* (Cancer the Crab) while *Shemesh* (Sun) and *Yareach* (Moon) are in free orbit and approaching the constellation of *Sarton the Holder* (Cancer the Crab)." Then the five magi and their apprentices stared into the night sky watching the blinking stars as if they were playing on the canvas back drop of black darkness. The night sound was very quiet with a slight cool breeze tickling the beards of the magi and combing through the hair of their apprentices.

As the Magi continued to watch the evening sky over the next two hours Mag Nbuwzaradan from Opis observed, "The path of *Shemesh* (Sun) and *Yareach* (Moon) is too low under the constellation of *Sartan the Holder.* If you would follow their projected trajectory it would make them pass through the constellation of *Ariy* (Leo the Lion) above the front feet." Then Mag Kadashman from Sippar added, "Yes, this would be true. It does not appear that they will stop in the constellation of *Sarton the Holder* (Cancer the Crab). With this being a possibility I propose that Mag Nbuwzaradan and I keep our eyes on *Shemesh* (Sun) and *Yareach* (Moon) while Magi Belsha'tstsar and Zabaia watch *Nogah the Bright* (Venus) and *Tsayar the Messenger* (Mercury). This would leave only *Tsadaq the Righteous* (Jupiter) for Master Magi Hammurabi to observe." All the Magi nodded their heads in agreement so Master Magi Hammurabi said, "Thank you Mag Kadashman for that suggestion. It appears that we are all in agreement. However I would add that the five apprentices watch closely *Regaleo* (Regulus) in the front feet of the constellation of *Ariy* (Leo the Lion) Yhuwdah (Judah) because this is the power for the throne." Once again all the Magi were in agreement so the five apprentices peeled their eyes upon the bright star of power *Regaleo* (Regulus).

All at once the five apprentices exclaimed, "Did you see that?" Then little seven-year old Marduk said, "Magi *Regaleo* (Regulus) has begun blinking with a brighter light!" Mag Kadashaman the expert in Hebrew astrology said, "The throne in the land of Yhuwdah (Judah) is beckoning for a change. Keep on the alert and watch brother Magi to the reaction of the stars. History is about to be written!"

Back in Yhuwdah (Judah) in the great city of Yruwshalaim (Jerusalem) many slumbered in their sleep as the night sky above them was telling a story. Beneath the stars the Vulture of Death continued to hover over the Palace of Herod with each new day lowering its circling patterns ever so slightly in order that the great city did not notice the serious condition of peril that the city was in. Yes, everyone was on edge and snapped at each other. Children seemed to get on the nerves of their parents and the parents on the nerves of each other. The consumption of fermented wine and alcohol had increased dramatically along with the confrontation between common citizens and the increased force of Roman soldiers on patrol. All blamed it on the nervousness of the upcoming *Chag HaCukkah*, Feast of Tabernacles and the forced family registration of the enrollment assessment. The unsuspecting citizens and early guests were not aware of the dark and evil force that hovered above them night and day drooling its saliva of hatred and discontent upon this great city.

As the *chag*, feast drew near King Herod the Great was tormented more and more in his sleep. Even now with his eyes closed, he feared and suspected everything and everyone of trying to kill him and take over his throne. Now two armed guards stood at the door inside his bedroom to keep watch instead of outside guarding the door entrance. They had to stand and watch as the demons tortured the mind of their king. He would physically toss and turn and even contort his body causing convulsions and foaming at the mouth. But tonight was different because his jerking was more violent. The stench of the odor emanating from his large body was overpowering even at times causing the guards to become nauseated and empty the contents of their stomachs into a latrine pot. Then all at once the king shouted out while in his sleep, "Help! Help me! He is coming to take my throne! Kill him!" Then he beat his fists and swung his arms wildly against the bed causing him to sweat profusely and increase the emission of the filthy stench from his body.

Long ago the palace physicians warned the palace staff that the paranoia and depression of King Herod the Great was compounded into a physical sickness appropriately called "Herod's Evil". The pain was excruciating the final years of his life. He had chronic kidney disease complicated by Fournier's gangrene. He also had scabies with visible worms crawling in his putrefied decaying flesh. A slow fire burned within him which was not so apparent to those who were in touch with him, but augmented his internal distress; for he had a terrible desire for food which it was not possible to resist. He was also affected with ulceration of the intestines with especially severe pain in the colon, while watery and transparent tumors settled about his feet and abdomen. The king also had trouble breathing and the odor of his breath was overwhelming. He suffered from convulsions in every limb which gave him uncontrollable strength. King Herod the Great literally became a demonic beast imprisoned by a human body of decaying flesh and bone. Thus the guards knew that it was just their duty to stand watch that no one came near him to cause him harm but not to keep him from harming himself because they themselves could be harmed with the uncontrollable demonic strength.

As King Herod tossed and turned in his sleep in Yhuwdah (Judah), the apprentices back in Babel (Babylon-modern Iraq) would exclaim each time *Regaleo* (Regulus) would blink with a brightening of light. The young boys even made a game of it by trying to outdo each other with the most magnificent sound to the much dismay of their masters, the Magi. The boys were doing their assigned task very diligently so the Magi learned to ignore the dramatic sound effects of the 'oos' and 'ahs' being produced by the vocal cords of the young boys. About the middle of the third watch of the night (around 1:30 a.m.), Magi Nbuwzaradan and Kadashman watched as *Shemesh* (Sun) and *Yareach* (Moon) enter the constellation of *Ariy* (Leo the Lion) Yhuwdah (Judah) through the back feet and pass over *Nogah the Bright* (Venus) and *Tsayar the Messenger* (Mercury) in the belly of *Ariy*.

This movement caused Magi Belsha'tstsar and Zabaia to utter, "*Nogah the Bright* (Venus) and *Tsayar the Messenger* (Mercury) just bowed their heads to *Shemesh* (Sun) and *Yareach* (Moon) but are staying positioned in the belly as the other two are passing over head." Then Master Magi Hammurabi reported, "Not much is happening with *Tsadaq the Righteous* (Jupiter). He is still in the claw of the constellation of *Sarton the Holder* (Cancer the Crab). As a matter of fact he hasn't even blinked one time the whole night."

Then at the end of the third watch (3 a.m.) Magi Nbuwzaradan and Kadashman noted, "*Shemesh* (Sun) and *Yareach* (Moon) have settled above the front feet in the mane of constellation *Ariy* (Leo the Lion) Yhuwdah (Judah). Directly below them in the front feet is *Regaleo* (Regulus) the scepter of king star." Within a half hour after this, Magi Belsha'tstsar and Zabaia remarked, "*Nogah the Bright* (Venus) and *Tsayar the Messenger* (Mercury) are on the move. It appears that as they are leaving the belly of *Ariy* and they are headed upwards to join *Shemesh* (Sun) and *Yareach* (Moon) in the mane above *Regaleo* (Regulus)." Mag Hammurabi remained silent but through discipline he kept a vigil eye on *Tsadaq the Righteous* (Jupiter) fighting off the temptation to take a look at the activity in the constellation of *Ariy* (Leo the Lion) Yhuwdah (Judah). About 4:00 a.m. the four stars of *Shemesh* (Sun), *Yareach* (Moon), *Nogah the Bright* (Venus) and *Tsayar the Messenger* (Mercury) clustered together above the front feet and the king star *Regaleo* (Regulus). *Shemesh* (Sun) was on the upper right and opposite it on the upper left was *Yareach* (Moon). Just below and between them was *Nogah the Bright* (Venus) and next to her was *Tsayar the Messenger* (Mercury). They appeared to form a very wide and flattened 'U' shape as if to form a crown above the king star *Regaleo* (Regulus). By now four of the apprentices had drifted off to sleep leaving little Marduk awake to keep an eye on the king star all by himself. Then at 5:00 a.m. *Tsadaq the Righteous* (Jupiter) began to faintly blink. Through his excitement Mag Hammurabi shouted, which woke up the four sleeping apprentices, "He blinked. The New King just blinked." Little by little, inch by inch *Tsadadq the Righteous* (Jupiter) the New King began to move with indications of leaving the claw of the constellation *Sarton the Holder* (Cancer the Crab). The Magi and their apprentices watched until dawn and the constellation and the stars could not be visibly seen any more. Then the Magi and their apprentices moseyed back to the home of Mag Hammurabi for some much needed rest after such a long watchful night.

Yowceph (Joseph) was awakened by the sound of a noisy rooster down the street. When he opened his eyes he was greeted by a soft pink and pale orange sky trying to breaking the darkness of the previous night. Today was the ninth day of *Tishri* (September), the day to begin the four and a half day journey to Beyth Lechem (Bethlehem) meaning 'house of bread' and the great city of Yruwshalaim (Jerusalem) meaning 'city of peace'. The thought of the excitement of these two cities stirred up the butterflies in his empty stomach. With a wide yawn and a big stretch he propelled himself off the straw mattress and headed down from the flat roof to the main floor. To his surprise his nose picked up the scent of frying eggs and fresh baking bread. As he followed the irresistible aroma that was tempting his empty stomach with tantalizing odors, he arrived in the kitchen area where he found Miryam (Mary) preparing breakfast.

Yowceph said, "What are you doing up already? You should be resting for a long day of travel." Miryam replied, "About an hour ago, the baby started kicking and I could not go back to sleep. You would think that He was in a hurry to get started and excited about *Chag HaCukkah*, the Feast of Tabernacles. Go back into the main room and I will bring breakfast to you shortly. I just about have it ready as soon as I finish peeling this fresh fruit." Yowceph (Joseph) complied with the request of Miryam (Mary) and sat down on the floor cushion in the main room. He looked up at the carvings on the two main beams depicting the struggles of mankind and his ancestors the Hebrew people. Then he began to ponder and daydream about the need for a New King to replace the lunatic King Herod the Great and win back the nation's independence from the Roman Empire.

8

Yowceph (Joseph) and Miryam (Mary) gathered their things after a quick breakfast and made their way to the front door. Yowceph lifted the wooden latch on the door and turned to guide Miryam out the door when their dark brown eyes met each other producing a grin on both of their faces. Miryam was first to cross the threshold followed closely behind by Yowceph. He closed the door and noticed Nathan ben Yow'ash and his wife, Tamar coming from up the street north. Yowceph gave them a quick wave and waited for them to arrive in front of his house. When they arrived, Yowceph said, "*Shalom.* What a beautiful day Yahuah has blessed us with for travel." Nathan replied, "*Shalom*, to you and your wife. I am glad we caught you before you left so that we can travel together. Shall we head out?" Then the four travelers headed south on the dusty road as they began the journey of a lifetime.

The plan today was to travel twenty-five miles as the crow flies and camp near the *Yardan River* (Jordan River) for the evening. It would actually be about a thirty-four mile journey as they descended down the hills from Nazareth southeast to the *Emek Yizre'el* (Jezreel Valley). *Emek Yizre'el* (Jezreel Valley) is a large fertile plain and inland valley south of the Lower Galilee region. This green fertile plain is covered with spread-out fields of wheat, cotton, sunflowers and corn. It is also home to vast grazing tracts full of multitudes of sheep and cattle. The name Yizre'el means 'Yahuah sows." According to Hebrew legend the valley once acted as the channel by which the Dead Sea located southeast of the valley was connected to the

Mediterranean Sea. Then the Great Flood changed the landscape forever. The highlands of *erets beniy gowlah,* land of the sons of captivity (Samaritans) border the valley from the south. To the west is Mount Carmel and to the east is *Emek Yardan* (Jordan Valley) just south of the *Sea of Chinneeth* (Sea of Galilee). Their camp for the night would be about six miles south of this prominent sea known for its great fishing industry and its unpredictable and rapid developing storms. The *Yardan River* (Jordan River) which flows from the *Sea of Chinneeth* (Sea of Galilee) would be their final destination for the day to make camp and rest for the night.

As they began the descent to the lush green valley just below, Nathan ben Yow'ash and his wife began singing the traditional travel song of *Chag HaCukkah,* Feast of Tabernacles. After a couple of notes Miyram (Mary) joined in with her beautiful soprano voice followed by Yowceph (Joseph) with his rich baritone voice. They sang the old Davidic song from the Holy Script found in 2 Shmuw" Yah (Samuel) chapter 7:18-29, ***"Who am I Oh Sovereign Yahuah and what is in my house that You have brought me to here? This was of no account in Your eyes Oh Sovereign Yahuah. But You have spoken an arrangement of words also to the house of Your servant concerning the future of a far off time. Is this the custom of me Oh Sovereign Yahuah? Because of Your spoken word on this matter and after Your heart of feelings and intellect You have done all this greatness to cause Your servant to know it. Therefore, You are great Oh Yahuah Yah, because there does not exist anything like you and there does not exist any Yah except You according to all this we have heard intelligently and paid attention to with our ears. Who is like Your people, like Yisra'Yah (Israel) one nation in the earth that Yahuah ascended out to redeem for Him a people and to make for Him a name and to do for You the great and frightening things for Your hand in front of the*** *faces of Your people whom You ransomed and preserved for You from Mitsrayim (Egypt) for foreign nations and their elohiym pagan gods?"*

The second stanza became more energetic and robust as the descent was naturally making them pick up the pace of their footsteps. **"You wrapped in Your arms for You Your people Yisra'Yah (Israel) to You for a people until the vanishing point of eternity. You Oh Yahuah have become and existed to them as Yah. At this time Oh Yahuah Yah the spoken word of this matter which You spoke in an arrangement of words about Your servant and about his house raise it up until the vanishing point of eternity and do as You have spoken in an arrangement of words. That Your name may be great until the vanishing point of eternity saying Yahuah of armies is Yah over Yisra'Yah (Israel). The house of Your servant David may exist as established in front of Your face. Because of You Oh Yahuah of armies, Yah of Yisra'Yah (Israel) have revealed in the ear of Your servant saying, 'I will build a house.' Therefore, Your servant has found graciousness in his heart to pray to You this supplication hymn. At this time, Oh Sovereign Yahuah You are Yah and Your spoken words of this matter exist as truth and You have spoken an arrangement of words to Your servant of this goodness. At this time let You assent and bless the house of Your servant to exist to the vanishing point of eternity in front of Your face, because You Oh Sovereign Yahuah have spoken an arrangement of words. Let the house of Your servants be blessed with Your benediction blessing to the vanishing point of eternity."**

At the end of the second stanza Miryam (Mary) grabbed her stomach with both hands and said, "Oh my goodness little one. Now is not the time to dance like your ancestor David. Now is the time for you to rest because we have a long way to go and mama doesn't need you trying to dance the *Hora Agadati* all by yourself."

The wife of Nathan ben Yow'ash said, "Do you think your little one knows we are about to approach the *Emek Yizre'el* (Jezreel Valley) and therefore is trying to do the famous Davidic dance known in this valley?" Miryam (Mary) laughed and replied, "I don't know. What I do know is that my belly is not big enough for the clapping of hands, kicking up the heels and twirling in circles for even the round dancing of this little one!" Yowceph (Joseph) interjected, "By the time the bright sun reaches its highest peak we should be resting in the *Emek Yardan* (Jordan Valley). Maybe the little one would like to grace us with lunch entertainment with its rendition of *HaTikvah* (The Hope), the song and dance of the upcoming *emek*, valley." The two women looked at each other and just rolled their eyes as if to politely ignore the dry humored comment by Yowceph (Joseph). However, the wife of Nathan ben Yow'ash rebuked, "Maybe if men had to carry a belly the size of a heavy watermelon around their waist instead of that light empty round thing on top of their necks, they would be less apt to tease a mother-to-be, eh?" Miryam (Mary) giggled as Yowceph (Joseph) turned red with embarrassment.

As they continued to walk through the *Emek Yizre'el* (Jezreel Valley) they could smell the fresh clover and the rich green shimmering grass. They listened to the dogs barking and the shepherds giving commands as the dogs worked to keep the herds of bleating sheep together. The sound of clanging neck bells jingled in the air as they passed herds of goats. The variety of colored goats against the green grass canvass created a beauty of its own. There were solid black, white and brown goats mixed with brown and black speckled white goats. Also, in the mix were black and brown stripped ones. Large herds of Simford (Israeli Red) cattle also dotted the grassy plain along the road in *Emek Yizre'el* (Jezreel Valley). Their brownish-red bodies with white faces and white underbellies added beauty to the already beautiful landscape.

This luscious fertile valley also created a picturesque beauty of many colorful wildflowers that were in bloom this time of the year. The men didn't seem to notice their beauty and chatted non-stop about the enrollment assessment, politics, the weather and other subjects that simply bored the women. However, Miryam (Mary) and Tamar, the wife of Nathan ben Yow'ash appreciated the beauty of Yahuah presented on the backdrop of the canvas of luscious green pastures. They would point out to each other as they recognized a particular varietal or color of flowers with their fragile petals.

The valley was dotted with patches of white Daisies with their bright yellow centers. Standing just above the green grass were the yellow Toothed Pheasants Eye and the red-orange Pheasants Eye. Here and there the women noticed the lavender star-like Hollyhocks and the Camel Grass with its lavender thin petals with a bright red tongue on top. Some of their favorites were the six-petal Dyers Bogloss with its brilliant blue large petals and the white six-petal star shaped Onion Weed with its pink stripe down the center of the petal. However, the ones that drew the most attention and even some picking were the Crown Anemone with its large multi-colored patches of red, light blue, pink, purple, violet, white and deep blue. These were also the favorite of many bees looking for pollen for their sweet nectar. Next to the yellow Field Marigolds were the dainty bright Snapdragons that also were added to the small hand bouquets of Miryam (Mary) and Tamar the wife of Nathan ben Yow'ash. All this array of color would soon be gone by the next new moon (month) because cooler temperatures would prevail with the upcoming winter rains and even snow in the upper elevations.

Just as the sun was reaching its highest peak in the sky, they were at the border of the *Emek Yardan* (Jordan Valley). The beginning group of four had now grown to a group of thirty sojourners. The travelers found a grove of Yhuwdah's Trees (Judah's) and settled down for a rest and some quick lunch alongside the road. This time of year the trees were in full bloom with its vast lilac colored blooms making them look like lavender umbrellas in this vast *emek,* valley. As Miryam (Mary) sat down her knap sack full of food, Yowceph (Joseph) began putting together the portable stool for Miryam to sit on. Those around him watched in awe as he put together this strange and never-seen-before contraption. When it was all together the men applauded and Miryam (Mary) looked in his direction in puzzlement. Then he parted the curious onlookers and carried the stool to Miryam (Mary) and said, "Here, my beautiful wife. Take a load off and enjoy your rest." Miryam (Mary) put her hands over her mouth in amazement and then replied, "My, oh my, aren't you the clever carpenter?" She sat down with the audience clapping and the other woman gathered around her to get a good look at this clever back saver.

Then Miryam (Mary) broke off a piece of her famous *Challah* bread loaf and gave it to Yowceph (Joseph). This special bread was made with six interwoven rope like strands made of white flour, water, and yeast. Miryam added honey and molasses for sweetener enhancement also with the addition of sweet raisons and cashews. Each strand was coated with an egg wash to help make it golden brown in baking. Before baking she topped it off with a mixture of poppy and sesame seeds for a robust flavor. They also nibbled on hardboiled eggs and date cakes as part of the lunch meal. Of course Miryam (Mary) would feel negligent if she did not get out the large container of cook's famous *haroset* dessert and the cloth bag of thin sweet bread wafer crackers to use for dipping into the delectable dessert. After an hour of eating and resting, it was time to begin the journey again in order to reach the campsite by sundown. Miryam busied herself repacking the food and Yowceph disassembled the portable wooden stool with many of the men inquiring about the possibility of procuring one just like it.

As they moved deeper into the *Emek Yardan* (Jordan Valley) they noticed a change in the scenery from the *Emek Yizre'el* (Jezreel Valley). The northern part of the *emek*, valley is several degrees warmer than the adjacent areas. Its fertile soils, plentiful water supply and year-round agricultural climate made the *Emek Yardan* (Jordan Valley) a key agricultural area exporting large amounts of fruit and vegetables all year-round. Instead of the virtually flat plain of lush glistening green pastures found in the *Emek Yizre'el* (Jezreel Valley) the *Emek Yardan* (Jordan Valley) had more trees in it. Some of the favorite trees of Miryam (Mary) were the Sweet Acacia Bush with its yellow-orange puff ball blossoms, the Syrian Maple with its silver-blue leaves or the Ground Pine with its yellow butterfly shaped leaves with tiny brown spots on them.

The group of thirty travelers stopped about the ninth hour (3 p.m.) for a quick rest and prayer time. They were only about seven miles from their destination for the day's journey. Yowceph (Joseph) got out the portable stool for Miryam (Mary) to sit on and rest as the men prepared for prayer time. After prayer time Miryam (Mary) lead the group in a quick Davidic hymn from the book of Thilahyim (Psalms) 17:5-8, "**My steps kept in Your tracks that my stroke have not wavered. I called on You because You will respond to me oh Yahuah. Depress Your ear to me and hear intelligently my spoken word of the matter. Distinguish Your kindness Oh Yahusha of those who flee to You for protection from those who rise up by Your right hand. Put a hedge of thorns about to guard and protect me as a pupil,** *the daughter of the eye in the shade of Your wings kept me secret."* At the conclusion of the song the group said in unison, "*Halal'Yah* (Hallelujah) meaning 'celebrate to Yahuah and shine His light." Then they got a drink of water, gathered their belongings and continued their journey towards the night camp before sunset arrived.

The group of travelers would stop briefly here and there as the local land owners were selling their fresh produce of onions, carrots, garlic, potatoes, celery, leeks, oranges, lemons, limes, strawberries, and various nuts. The busy road virtually became a smorgasbord of an endless farmers market. This was an advantage to the land owners because the travelers were in a hurry and didn't spend much time haggling over the prices set by the land owners. Miryam (Mary) only purchased a few fresh carrots to munch on for that evening's meal. She had packed enough food to last the entire four and a half day trip to the great city of Yruwshalaim (Jerusalem).

About sixty-five miles south of the group of travelers in the great city of Yruwshalaim (Jerusalem) Matityahu ben Levi and *Qatan Yow* (Little Joe) arrived at the Gennath Gate after registering for the enrollment assessment and concluding the mining business with the Roman officials. Waiting at the gate were six fully armed Roman soldiers who were diligently checking passes of those attempting to enter into the Upper City. Standing off to the right side was the famous fan maker, Ya'kov Melek'Beyth Aer (James Henry Ayers) and his ten year old son Chizqiy (Charles). When Ya'kov noticed Matityahu above the crowd mounted on his black stallion, he began to walk towards Matityahu and *Qatan Yow* (Little Joe). Then he began to yell above the hustle and bustle, "Matityahu ben Levi, *Shalom*." Matityahu ben Levi and *Qatan Yow* (Little Joe) dismounted their horses and began to walk towards Ya'kov's voice. Matityahu ben Levi and Ya'kov grasped each other's right forearms and kissed each other on both cheeks as was the customary greeting. Then Ya'kov said, "Yowceph ben Matityahu I assume. My how you have grown! Meet my son Chizqiy (Charles)." The two boys nodded at each other as they remained at the sides of their fathers with *Qatan Yow* (Little Joe) hanging tightly onto the reigns of his horse.

Ya'kov, the fan maker said, "Matityahu ben Levi it is so good to see you once again. Here are your passes into the Upper City. Let's go on through the gates and head to the house. My wife has made some fresh lemonade and sweet raison cakes to greet you." The Roman soldiers looked over the passes and allowed Matityahu and Qatan Yow (Little Joe) to pass with their horses in tow. Chizqiy (Charles) was now walking by Qatan Yow (Little Joe) and said, "Is that your own horse, Yowceph (Joseph)." Qatan Yow (Little Joe) said, "Yes, all mine and please call me Qatan Yow (Little Joe)." "Ok, Qatan Yow (Little Joe), what is the name of your horse?" questioned ten year old Chizqiy (Charles). Qatan Yow answered, "His name is Eliysha (Elijah) after the great prophet." "Do you think I could ride him?" begged Chizqiy (Charles). Qatan Yow said, "Sure. I don't care. Give me your foot." Then he hefted Chizqiy upon the back of Eliysha (Elijah) and Chizqiy grabbed a hold of the mane for a handle as Qatan Yow (Little Joe) held onto the reigns and lead the new rider down the cobblestone street. Matityahu ben Levi turned his head and then replied, "Looks like the two boys are going to get along just fine. Qatan Yow (Little Joe) will enjoy this trip since he has someone his own age to play with."

The other travelers to the north of Yruwshalaim (Jerusalem) in the Northern *Emek Yardan* (Jordan Valley) now had their eyes fixed upon their campsite for the evening in the distance. It was a small grove of oak trees about two hundred yards from the Yardan River (Jordan River). This was the perfect spot off the main dirt road. The trees would provide much needed firewood for the evening campfires and their branches would provide protection from the night dew or unexpected moisture. Of course the river would provide water for cooking and watering the thirsty camels and donkeys. The open space just beyond the trees would provide an area for the children to play under the watchful eye of their mothers. Nathan ben Yow'ash, his wife, Yowceph (Joseph) and Miryam (Mary) quickly selected their spot and Nathan ben Yow'ash went to gather firewood as Yowceph (Joseph) helped get their campsite set up for the evening. The women began to prepare the evening meal and the men joined the other men of the group to make traveling plans for the following day.

When the evening meal was ready the men returned to their own campsites and Yowceph (Joseph) gave the thanksgiving prayer over the food that they were about to consume. He also thanked Yahuah for a very successful first day of travel and asked for good travel mercies for the following day. He noticed Miryam (Mary) looked tired but she continued to chatter a mile-a-minute with the wife of Nathan ben Yow'ash. The sun sat in an array of burnt orange, red and deep blues. It was not long before the stars began to twinkle above their heads in the black sky. More than a dozen campfires provided a perfect ambiance for storytelling and the eyes of the smaller children to grow heavy and fall asleep for the night. Soon, too the adults found themselves yearning to join the smaller ones in dreamland because they were weary from their daylong journey. As Miryam (Mary) was drifting off to sleep all she could think about was getting back to her hometown.

That very night in the eastern city of Babel in the country of Babel (Babylon-modern Iraq), the faithful night-watchers were gathered with their eyes scanning the vast evening sky of blinking lights. Master Magi Hammurabi reminded everyone, "Last night

Tsadaq the Righteous (Jupiter) New King was moving and heading out of the claw of the constellation of *Sarton the Holder* (Cancer the Crab). In the constellation of *Ariy* (Leo the Lion) Yhuwdah (Judah) forming an upward semi-circle in the shoulder mane above the King Star *Regaleo* (Regulus) in the upper left position is *Yareach* (Moon), lower left is *Tsayar the Messenger* (Mercury), lower right is *Nogah the Bright* (Venus) and in the upper right position is *Shemesh* (Sun). Tonight we are watching to see if the four stars remained grouped and also watch the movement of *Tsadaq the Righteous* (Jupiter)."

Then little seven-year old Marduk just could not contain himself, "But Master Hammurabi you left out watching *Regaleo* (Regulus). Someone must watch the King Star to see if it grows brighter and with your permission I would volunteer for this mighty important task." Mag Hammurabi grew a little impatient with his young apprentice showing off rebuffed, "Fine, Marduk you watch the King Star while the rest of us will watch possibly history in the making. However, I don't want to hear one word. Not even one mere peep come out of your mouth when you miss the show. Do you understand me!" "Yes, master," shrinking in rebuke answered little Marduk. Then he thought to himself, "*I just know all the action will be centered around the King Star. I just know it from the Hebrew Holy Writ.*" He let out a big sigh and glued his little eyes upon the scepter star in the front feet of the constellation of *Ariy* (Leo the Lion) Yhuwdah (Judah). Then he felt a hand on his shoulder and a familiar voice saying, "Can I watch with you Marduk?" It was his best friend Meyshak, the apprentice of Mag Kadashman from the town of Sippar. Marduk replied, "Sure."

At the end of the first night watch, around 9 p.m. *Tsadaq the Righteous* (Jupiter) New King moved out of the upper claw of the constellation of *Sarton the Holder* (Cancer the Crab) and began the journey across the dark sky towards the next constellation which was

99

Ariy (Leo the Lion) Yhuwdah (Judah). As soon as the New King had completely left the constellation, Marduk and Meyshak exclaimed, "Did you see that?" Then they counted out loud, "One….Two…. Three….Four" Mag Besha'tstsar from Nippur questioned, "What are your two up too?" Apprentice Meyshak blurted, "Go ahead Marduk. Tell him. Tell everyone what just happened." Mag Zabaia from the town of Erek responded, "Yes, young Marduk share with all of us what you two have seen." Little Marduk cleared his throat as if he was taking the stage in a famous oratory and said, "Esteemed Magi and fellow apprentices, my fellow observer Meyshak and I just witnessed *Regaleo* (Regulus) King Star blinking brightly not once, not twice but four separate and distinct times when *Tsadaq the Righteous* (Jupiter) New King exited out of the constellation of *Sarton the Holder* (Cancer the Crab)."

Master Mag Hammurabi, his master stated, "Why do you always have to be so dramatic? This observation may have significant meaning….." At this point the two youngest boys were grinning from ear to ear since they had volunteered to watch the King Star in the front feet of the constellation of *Ariy* (Leo the Lion) Yhuwdah (Judah). Then Mag Hammurabi looked directly at the two proud observers and continued, "…Yet on the other hand it may mean nothing at all. However, it must be noted as an observation. Only time will tell if it has meaning or not." The rest of the evening was uneventful with only *Tsadaq the Righteous* (Jupiter) New King on the move inching further away from the constellation of *Sarton the Holder* (Cancer the Crab) and traveling ever closer to the constellation of *Ariy* (Leo the Lion) Yhuwdah (Judah).

9

The next morning, which began day two of their journey to the great city of Yruwshalaim (Jerusalem), the sleepy travelers in the camp were awakened at dawn just as the dark eastern sky was beginning to show a sliver of pink and orange colors. Their awakening was sudden and with great alarm. There was a loud and banging noise traveling rapidly throughout the slumbering camp accompanied by wild screaming. Men began to grab their swords and daggers, the women cradled their sobbing and terrified children and the frightened camels and donkeys were trying to break their tie downs to escape the disturbing raucous. The noisy enemy wasted no time in traveling throughout the entire camp running over and near the alarmed travelers. There was not enough morning light to see who the perpetrators were but the trail of their sound was distinct and easy to track. After fifteen minutes of total disruption of the camp the enemy was captured and seized by a handful of armed men. Then above the crying children laughter could be heard from the men and women. The perpetrator seemed to be a lone curious wild goat who had gotten a satchel of copper pots and pans hooked around its neck and could not relive them to escape the noisy attachment clinging around its neck. After the terrified wild goat was relived of its noisy contraption the travelers decided that they were wide awake so they began to breakdown camp and get started down the road towards their distant destination of the great city Yruwshalaim (Jerusalem).

Today's journey would take them eight miles south of the city known in the Hellene (Greek) language as Scythopolis meaning 'City of the Sythians". Sythians were nomadic Persian (Iranian) tribes ruled by Chieftains who were hired mercenaries as soldiers motivated by greed and the love of money. The Hebrew people called the city Beyth Sh'an meaning 'City of Ease". It was located at the junction of the southern *Emek Yardan* (Jordan River Valley) and the eastern *Emek Yizre'el* (Jezreel Valley) essentially controlling access from the interior to the coast as well as from the great city of Yruwshalaim (Jerusalem) to the territory of Galilee. This city was the place of major historical events in the annuals of Hebrew history. The first important historical reference involved the first king of the Hebrew people.

As they were walking south on the dusty road Yowceph (Joseph) turned to Miryam (Mary) and said, "You know we will be passing by important ruins of our Hebrew heritage today. Beyth Sh'an (Sycthopolis) is the place where the dead body of King Sha'uwl (Saul) and his sons were hung by the Plishtiy (Philistines). It was recorded in the Holy Writ in the book of 1 Shmuw'Yah (1 Samuel) Chapter 31:8-10, *"It came to pass on the next day that the Plishtiy (Philistines) inhabitants came to strip and plunder the pierced to death and they found Sha'uwl (Saul) and his three sons fallen on Mountain Gilboa. They cut off his head and stripped off his weapons and sent it out and away into the land of the Plishtiy (Philistines) inhabitants all around to announce the glad news for the house of their idols and the people. They put his weapons in the house of ashtarowth (ashtaroth) and his body they fastened by driving nails through on the wall of protection of the city of Beyth Sh'an."* Miryam (Mary) looked back at Yowceph (Joseph) and said, "Yes, dear I remember."

After a few moments of silence, Miryam (Mary) spoke up. "Yowceph not only did this city usher in the rule of our great ancestral king David but members of my family were murdered here." Yowceph was taken aback and said, "Really? Who?" Miryam answered, "My great-great-great-great-great uncle King Yownathan (Jonathan) Maccabim the oldest son of Matityahu ben Yowchanan (John) Maccabim, the leader of the 'Great Maccabim Revolt' against the tyranny and contempt of the Helene (Greek) ruling government against our Yah Yahuah." Yowceph in surprise requested, "Really, I did not know that! Tell me more."

Miryam (Mary) continued to tell the story, "Grandfather Matityahu ben Levi told me this story in private many times as I was growing up when he would come and visit me at the orphanage in the synagogue at the great city of Yruwshalaim (Jerusalem). He warned me never to repeat it until I was a grown woman and had a family of my own to teach it to my children. Even then my family is to keep this information amongst ourselves because of its political ties against Rome and especially the Herod family." Yowceph looked around at the other travelers to make sure no one could hear their conversation and then he put his index finger to his lips and said, "It will be our little secret that will only be shared with our children and their children. Please continue."

Miryam (Mary) answered, "Yownathan (Jonathan) Maccabim was known as 'The Diplomat' and ruled the Hebrew nation for nineteen years of great prosperity. He had established a good relationship with the government in Rome and was generally at peace with the government in Antioch, Syria. However, an evil ruler, General Diodotus Tryphon lured King Yownathan (Jonathan) and his sons into a trap at the city of Acre. This city was the garrison stronghold of the Helen (Greek) rule on the Mediterranean Coast and had been promised to be released to the Hebrew Maccabim family many times. Once again word was sent to King Yownathan

Maccabim that this city was going to be released to the Hebrew people as he was returning from a great victory in the northern territories. Therefore, King Yownathan and his sons along with a small army stopped by the city on their way home to Yruwshalaim (Jerusalem). As soon as the city gates were closed a rain of arrows fell upon the small delegation of the Hebrew entourage leaving only King Yownathan and his sons alive. General Diodotus Tryphon sent word to Yruwshalaim (Jerusalem) to the king's brother, Shim'own (Simon) demanding a large ransom. Shim'won did not take the bait of the ransom demands and instead rallied a crushing army. General Diodotus Tryphon emptied and abandoned the garrison retreating back to Antioch, Syria. However, a heavy snow fell and stopped the hasty retreat. Knowing he could not defeat Shim'own and his army, he murdered Yownathan and his sons and put them in shallow graves with markers as a ploy hoping that when seeing the markers Shim'own would call off the hunt and grieve for his brother and nephews. However, it had the opposite effect and the Hebrew army caught the Helene (Greek) army and destroyed them before they could reach Antioch, Syria. It was at Beyth Sh'an that Yownathan and his sons were murdered and buried in shallow graves." Yowceph (Joseph) remained silent just shaking his head as they continued on their journey south.

After traveling a couple of miles Yowceph broke the silence and said to Miryam, "I am going to go up ahead and talk to Nathan ben Yow'ash. I will send Tamar back to keep you company." "Oh I am ok Yowceph. I am really enjoying the scenery. However, if Tamar doesn't want to listen to the heavy conversation between two men, just let her know that I am available company for a peaceful sanctuary," replied Miryam. Yowceph (Joseph) let out a light chuckle and squeezed her shoulder gently and lovingly. Then he proceeded to pick up the pace to catch Nathan ben Yow'ash about fifteen yards ahead of him. As soon as he caught up to Nathan ben Yow'ash, Miryam (Mary) watched as Tamar threw up both of her arms and shook her head from side to side. Tamar stopped immediately in her tracks and turned around to wait for Miryam (Mary) to approach.

When Miryam (Mary) got to within speaking distance Tamar said, "You really appreciate good woman folk when two men get together to conquer the world with their endless conversations and macho bravado when they try to tell a bigger story than the other." Both women broke out into laughter as Tamar joined the side of Miryam (Mary) and began walking down the dusty trail with her. Miryam noticed that Yowceph (Joseph) turned his head to make sure she was alright and gave her a little nod before returning to the heated conversation of the day with Nathan ben Yow'ash. Tamar then asked, "How are you and the little one holding up?" Miryam (Mary) replied, "Oh just fine. I love the fresh air and scenery and the baby seems to sleep as we travel. But boy when it is time for me to rest, that little one moves into a thousand different positions poking my ribs here and there and kicking up a storm."

Tamar questioned, "I know that you were originally from the great city of Yruwshalaim (Jerusalem). This will be my first trip to the wonderful city. Would you please tell me what it is like? I mean if it is ok and does not bring back bad memories." Miryam (Mary) obliged, "Oh, Tamar it is such a big and marvelous city filled with such wonders and amazement that your wildest dreams could not even comprehend." "Don't stop! Tell me more. Tell me everything including the smallest of details!" begged Tamar full of curiosity. Miryam (Mary) with excitement in the tone of her voice began describing the great city of Yruwshalaim (Jerusalem) to Tamar.

"I know the thing that will interest you the most is the vast marketplace of hundreds upon hundreds of souks with every kind of trinket and object your mind would ever conceive. The food market is lined up as far as your eyes can see with an endless assortment of colorful fresh vegetables and fruits. Red, green and yellow apples are on tables in perfect rows joined by rows of oranges, yellow bananas, green limes, deep purple plums, brown dates, yellow lemons, heaps of dried raisons, purple grapes and yellow grapefruit. There are countless tables of stacked yellow pineapples with green tops, green kiwi and yellow pawpaw fruit surrounded by tables with heaped containers of red strawberries, blueberries, blackberries, watermelon, rose colored pomegranates and multi-colored mangos. The colored montage continues with red tomatoes, tan potatoes, green broccoli, bright deep-orange carrots, green cucumbers, orange pumpkins, yellow squash, red and green and yellow bell peppers white cauliflower, green spinach and lettuce, green and black olives and mounds of yellow, red and tan onions."

As they walked Miryam (Mary) continued, "Your sight is not the only thing that is dazzled but your nose is tantalized by the vast spice market. There are baskets upon baskets of round black pepper, yellow mustard seed, minty smelling triangle-shaped cardamom with its dark brown color, sweet dark tan ginger root with its protruding appendages, fresh bright green coriander with it parsley shaped leaves or the small round dried coriander seed with its light brown colors. These aromas are mixed with turmeric with its sweet mustardy smell and yellow color sitting next to the cumin with its oblong shape and yellow-brown color with white stripes emitting its strong earthy and warm scent. Not far away is the red-brown sweet smelling nutmeg tucked in between the paprika made from dried bright red bell peppers not to be outdone by the strong dark brown elongated sweet cloves and fresh cinnamon sticks or the brown ground warm and sweet smelling cinnamon powder. The pungent aroma from these vast spices takes your mind away from the heavy woes of the world."

"Right next to the spice market is the fresh flower market full of aromatic lavender and beautiful double petal roses arranged like a giant rainbow of reds, yellows, pinks, violets, oranges, and whites casting their sweet smell into the air. The isles of the streets come alive with the color of blue bonnets, red poppies, purple orchids, multiple colors of tulips, my sister's favorite white Shulamit's comb, pink and white pishta, white daisies with their yellow centers, hundreds of colors of iris, yellow chrysanthemums, buttercups and of course the very beautiful Lily of the Sharon and many more beautiful and delicate flowers to even mention."

The mesmerized Tamar was awe struck but then grabbed her nose and said, "That sure beats the downdraft from those foul smelling camels upwind from us! They smell almost as bad as their master do! Those beasts sure make you watch your step to avoid stepping in one of their road deposits." Then Miryam added, "Yeah and you have to watch behind the camels too." Tamar and Miryam (Mary) burst out in laughter and giggled so loud it brought backward glances from Yowceph (Joseph) and Nathan ben Yow'ash. After they gained control of themselves, Tamar said, "Oh Miryam (Mary) the great city sounds so wonderful already but what about the shopping? Tell me about the shops in the market district. What can I expect to see?"

Miryam continued her oral tour of the market district, "Well, there are shops for everything you would ever want to see. There are fabric shops with draping rich blue, royal purple, deep red and pure white silk and sheers. Countless jewelry shops line both sides of the streets bursting with shimmering gold bracelets, anklets, necklaces and rings. Many pottery shops are there to lure your money out of your hand with exquisite artwork on them along with vases of marble, onyx and ivory. It appears as an endless glimmering sea of shiny copper in various shapes and sizes. Thousands of trinket shops are available to sell you anything you want and of course during these festival days when the streets will be crowded with plenty of buyers the merchants will be demanding outlandish prices. I am going to warn you that these merchants are very shrewd and can see a country girl like you coming from a mile away. They will convince you that you can't live another day without their wares at such bargain prices with a very short supply and a huge demand so their wares won't last long and are such a rare find. My advice is that you convince yourself that you have everything you need or they will part you with all your money and leave you broke with worthless stuff that you can't even trade. Of course I haven't even mentioned the exotic animal market, the fresh meat market, the human slave market, the nut market, the rug market or the furniture market. Yruwshalaim (Jerusalem) is the capital of the world regardless of what Rome thinks. It is truly a great city of endless wonders and of course the Holy Temple is a sight to behold. It will be an experience that you will remember for the rest of your life."

The morning time had flown by and the miles traveled seemed short by Miryam (Mary) giving Tamar a synopsis of the market district of the great city Yruwshalaim (Jerusalem). Now the small caravan was stopping and gathering along the side of the dusty road for nourishment and to parch their thirsty throats with water. The sun was at its highest peak in the sea of blue cloudless sky above thus it was time for the noon meal. Yowceph (Joseph) as usual unpacked his portable stool invention for Miryam (Mary) to sit on and rest. Lunch would be very quick today because they had to reach the city of Beyth Sh'an before the ninth hour (3:00 p.m.) afternoon prayers. Miryam (Mary) and Yowceph (Joseph) quickly downed a couple of raison cakes, small chunks of cheese and a boiled egg. Within forty-five minutes the small caravan was once again on the move southward on the dusty trail towards their destination of the great city Yruwshalaim (Jerusalem).

About the ninth hour (3:00 p.m.) they reached the city of Beyth Sh'an known in the Helene (Greek) language as Scythopolis just in time for afternoon prayers. As they approached the outside wall of the city, Miryam (Mary) reached down and grabbed the hand of Yowceph (Joseph) and held on to it tightly. Yowceph turned to her and gently said, "What is the matter? Are you all right?" Miryam answered, "Yes, I'm ok. I am just a little uneasy as I think about the headless and lifeless body of *Melek* Sha'uwl (King Saul) and his sons hanging on this very wall. His son Yownathan (Jonathan) was such a dear and close friend to our ancestor the Great *Melek* David (King David). Then to think many years later another great Hebrew *melek*, king, was ruthlessly and needlessly murdered in this very spot, my own kin of *Melek* (King) Yownathan Maccabim. It is as if their blood is crying out to me from the very wooden beams and particles of brown soil that drank their life blood. Even the innocent baby in my protective womb is restless as if it can sense the barbaric death of a blameless life."

Yowceph (Joseph) gently squeezed her hand in return and replied, "Come on let's hurry inside the wood gates of the city with the others. We will only be here a short time to pray and in two and a half hours we will be at our evening campsite eight miles south of here." He led Miryam (Mary) to the rest of the women and produced the portable stool. When she was settled he joined the rest of the men heading to the local synagogue for prayer. Miryam (Mary) did not participate with the other women in their rambling chit-chat but rather rested and when approached about her silence, she simply replied that she was just tired and enjoying the brief time to rest before another two and a half hour walk. However, inside she was exploding with uneasiness of the strange feeling of somehow the historical evidence of this city's reputation of murdering Hebrew *melek*, kings, was a threat of a barbaric death to her innocent unborn child. The restlessness and stirring of the baby in her protective womb produced severe heartburn and she could not get comfortable.

Soon the men returned from the synagogue and one by one the small caravan exited the city gates and continued to head south on the dusty trail towards their evening campsite. About a mile out of the city the baby once again became at rest and mother's severe heartburn receded. Her clammy hands became dry and her usual smile once again appeared on her face. She released the hand of Yowceph (Joseph) and he said, "You must be feeling better again." Miryam replied, "Yes, that was the strangest thing that I have ever experienced. I have not had those feelings since the needless death of my father being murdered by Herod and watching my mother die from grief. What I can't figure out is how the baby seemed to know about the threat of death to Hebrew *melek*, kings. Why did it feel threatened? The baby felt as if it was in danger of a brutal and barbaric death." Yowceph (Joseph) took a deep breath and let out a big sigh and responded in a caring and soft tone, "I don't know Miryam (Mary). I was warned by my mother and even cook that the emotions of a woman with child run the gamut of one extreme to another. We men are not to try to figure them out or even question why but rather flow with the tide and not cause waves. I am not saying that your feelings were not real but rather that the tide of your uneasiness has come and gone and now it is time to deal in the moment of you feeling your cheerful and wonderful self. You said yourself that the baby is at peace now so let's just focus on that and not invite back unnecessary grief where grief is not wanted." Miryam (Mary) reached up and gently tapped the center of his forehead and said, "Oh, wonderful husband how did you get so smart and wise beyond your years?" Yowceph (Joseph) let out a brief chuckle and replied, "It's not my wisdom or intelligence but rather my resolute faith knowing that the three of us are in the all mighty protective hands of Yahuah. If He is for us, who can be against us?" Miryam (Mary) lifted her head towards the sea of blue sky and said, "*Halal Yah*, Celebrate to Yahuah." They looked into each other's deep brown eyes, smiled and gave each other a nod of agreement.

Two and a half hours later they arrived at their evening campsite which was at the junction of the southern *Emek Yardan* (Jordan River Valley) and the eastern *Emek Yizre'el* (Jezreel Valley). They would be nestled in the great valley between two mountain ranges. Therefore the men of the caravan hustled to gather wood for the evening campfires as the sun would quickly set behind the western range of hills. The women began preparing for the evening meal and those with small children got them settled down in the camp. The older children were allowed to play and release their stored up energy prior to the evening meal but had to remain close under the watchful eyes of their mothers. Most of the children chased fireflies while others played tag and wrestled. Soon the camp was organized as the darkness of the night settled in all around them. After the evening meal the older men told ancient stories as the weary eyed children listened intently until their heavy eyelids gently eased shut and they drifted off into the deep restful sleep of dreamland for the night. As the embers of the campfire glowed red and the flames grew small Tamar said, "Well, we are half way there. After Miryam described the great city I just can't wait to get to the wondrous marketplace. It will be a dream come true." Quickly her husband

Nathan ben Yow'ash replied, "And that my witnesses, is exactly why I have control of the purse strings and she maintains possession of her dreams!" Tamar gave Nathan ben Yow'ash a teasing jab in his ribs with her finger as the remaining spectators around the campfire roared with laughter. Then everyone got ready to go to bed and Yowceph (Joseph) and Miryam (Mary) silently watched the blinking stars in the canvas of darkness of the evening sky far above them until they too drifted off to a peaceful and restful sleep.

Also, that night back in the territory and city of Babel (Babylon-modern Iraq) Master Magi Hammurabi had gathered his faithful night-watchers to peer into the darkened canvas of the night filled with twinkling lights of the evening stars. *Yareach* the moon, *Tsayar the Messenger* (Mercury), *Nogah the Bright* (Venus), and *Shemesh* the sun were still gathered in the shoulder area of the constellation of *Ariy* (Leo the Lion) Yhuwdah (Judah) forming a flattened semi-circle a distance above *Regaleo* (Regulus) the bright king star. The previous night, *Tsadaq the Righteous* (Jupiter) New King had departed from the constellation of *Sarton the Holder* (Cancer the Crab) and began inching towards the constellation of *Ariy* (Leo the Lion) Yhuwdah (Judah). By the end of the third watch of the night (3:00 a.m.), *Tsadaq the Righteous* (Jupiter) New King had entered the back feet of the constellation of *Ariy* (Leo the Lion) Yhuwdah (Judah) and was moving ever so slowly.

The three apprentices Shadrak, Abed Ngow and Gungunam had long ago lost interest in the slow movement and after chasing fireflies had fallen asleep by the campfire. Only apprentices Meyshak and seven-year old Marduk remained vigilant with the five Magi in watching history in the making. At the end of the forth watch (6:00 a.m.) the morning dawn began to break the darkness of the night in the eastern sky making it difficult to see the movement of the slow moving *Tsadaq the Righteous* (Jupiter) New King inching ever so slowly in the valley between the back feet of *Ariy* (Leo the Lion) Yhuwdah (Judah). Magi Nbuwzaradan from the town of Opis, Belsha'tstsar from the town of Nippur and Zabaia from the town of Erech woke up their soundly sleeping apprentices. Then the ten night-watchers journeyed down the hill towards the city of Babel to journal their nightly data and get some rest at the home of Mag Hammurabi before the next evening of night-watching.

10

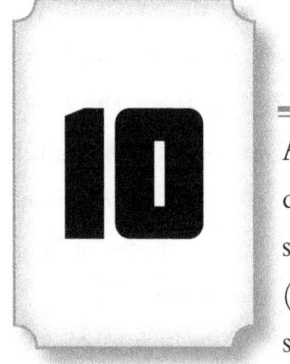

As the dawn continued from the east in the country of Babel (Babylon-modern Iraq) and stretch to the west over the *Emek Yardan*, (Jordan River Valley) a sliver of the morning sun could barely be seen peeking above the eastern hills. The ball of fire was just a sliver and was completely surrounded by multi-colored hues of pinks and oranges creating a spectacular greeting as a good-morning signature from Creator Yahuah. The crisp morning air was filled with the smell of a fresh dew mixed with a tinge of smoke escaping from the white ashes of a few lasting campfires from the night before. A faint stirring sound could be heard as the first to be awakened began to greet the sunrise with wide open eyes. The stirring sound increased in pace and sounds as many more were awakened to the new day. By now the ball of fire in the east was no longer a small sliver but was showing half of its splendor changing the hue of the sky to yellow and red-orange. A few clouds could be seen in the eastern horizon above the hills which were a dark steel blue gray. Finally, within a few moments the entire camp was a buzz scurrying here and there to get packed for the day's journey south to the great city.

Today the small caravan would finish traveling through the eastern *Emek Yizre'el* (Jezreel Valley) and enter into *HaMidbar Yhuwdah*, the Desert of Judah. Therefore, the caravan leader gathered all the men near and made an announcement, "Men please pay close attention to what I am about to tell you for the safety of your women and children. The destination for the campsite for this evening will be ten miles north of the great walled city of *Yriychow* (Jericho). Today's journey will be the toughest of all as we must climb thirty-five hundred feet in elevation through *HaMidbar Yhuwdah*, the Desert of Judah. The natural tendency would be to slow down and rest but please for the safety and welfare of your family encourage them to push on. Robbers and thieves hide in the treacherous rocky hills and white chalk caves to pick you off one by one. It is imperative that we all stick together and no one can afford to lag behind. I will not slow down the caravan or make unnecessary stops for the lagging behind and weary as it will only jeopardize the safety and welfare of the entire caravan. Do I make myself perfectly clear on this matter? We will be leaving in half an hour." All the men responded with a resounding, *ken-ken,* yes-yes and each returned back to their own campsite to gather their families.

 Miryam (Mary) met Yowceph (Joseph) with a broad smile and gave him a small kiss on the cheek as she handed him his cloak that she had been using for extra warmth during the rather cool evening night. He put it on and then reached down to pick up his backpack that contained the special chair for Miryam. Then all of a sudden Yowceph began beating his chest, waving his arms wildly and dancing like a maniac in one place. Miryam placed both of her hands over her mouth and giggled. By now half of those near the couple were watching in disbelief and the other half were laughing uncontrollably at the wild and chaotic sight of Yowceph. With a great burst of energy Yowceph wildly flung off his cloak launching it air born towards the heavens. The cloak went one way and a little fur ball the size of a lemon flew the opposite direction. Both the cloak and the little fur ball hit the hard ground landing simultaneously about six feet from each other. The dazed and frightened creature scampered as fast as its miniscule legs could carry it away from all the commotion. You see, unknown to Yowceph, Miryam had caught and hid a small field mouse in the inside pocket of his cloak. Miryam (Mary) quickly said between giggles, "Yowceph dear, do think the poor little creature will be ok?" This brought another round of laughter from the onlookers and just left Yowceph speechless breathing hard with his hands on his hips. Then the group one by one began to step onto the main dusty road to begin the day's journey south to the great city of Yruwshalaim (Jerusalem). Miryam continued to play innocent by taking the strong arm of Yowceph (Joseph) as they began to travel south with the rest of the caravan and he never suspected his mischievous wife.

By the third hour that morning (9 a.m.) the small caravan had passed out of the southern *Emek Yardan* (Jordan River Valley) and even the eastern *Emek Yizre'el* (Jezreel Valley) and into the wondrous *HaMidbar Yhuwdah*, the Desert of Judah. Miryam (Mary) who had become the self-appointed tour guide for Tamar the wife of Yownathan ben Yow'ash (Jonathan son of Joash) their traveling companions from Nazareth. So she began her narrative of what to expect to see and learn during the traveling for this day. She began, "This evening our destination will be ten miles north of the fortified city of Yriychow (Jericho). It is called the City of Palm Trees in our native Hebrew tongue and is thought to derive from the old Canaanite word *Yareach*, meaning moon since the city was an early center of worship for their pagan lunar deities. As you know this famous city was demolished by our ancient leader Yhowshuwa (Joshua) with the blast of the shofar ram's horns and the almighty power of Yahuaeh as our forefathers entered into this great Promised Land."

"Today I want you to observe the vast fields of sugarcane and bananas. The best of all the sugar in the known world is made here. Our journey today will take us through breathtaking views that will constantly change between mountains, cliffs, and white chalk hills that stand alongside plateaus, riverbeds and of course the ever famous deep canyons. We will sip cool water from ancient oases' and rest in the shade of its broad palm trees creating a refreshing atmosphere of cool air." At that moment Yowceph (Joseph) quipped, "That sure will be a welcome relief from the current hot air we are experiencing!" Then Miryam (Mary) and Tamar shot daggered looks back to him with their deep brown eyes that could silence a rumbling volcano. Yowceph quickly stammered, "*Lo!Lo!,* No, no that is not what I meant. I was referring to the heat of the rising sun as we pass through this *midbar*, desert." Yownathan ben Yow'ash shook his head and laughingly said, "Give it up old boy while you are ahead because you are so busted." The anxious audience of Tamar begged, "Oh, Miryam don't pay those two oafs any mind. Please continue, I want to hear more."

Then Miryam (Mary) after clearing her throat continued, "Well we won't be passing through them on our path but this *midbar*, desert has miles and miles of great white sand dunes that are simply breathtaking except during a sandstorm of course. The *midbar*, desert is known for its rugged landscape, which has provided a refuge and hiding place for rebels and zealots throughout history, as well as solitude and isolation to devoted priests and hermits. During the days of the influential and powerful Maccabim family, large fortresses such as Massada and Horkenya were established in this *midbar*, desert as military strongholds. As we continue to travel I will point out to you the vast beauty held in this magnificent *Midbar Yhuwdah,* Desert of Judah. When we reach camp we will only be a day and a half journey from the great city of Yruwshalaim, (Jerusalem)." Miryam ceased her narrative because the caravan leader had signaled to stop and he said, "Don't get to comfortable this is only a brief fifteen minute stop and then we must push on!"

Just as the caravan was ready to travel once again after their brief rest, a group of about two dozen wild Onyx ran past them. These spectacular creatures sprinted by the small caravan with grace and beauty. Their black and brown speckled faces outlined their massive pure white bodies that showed off their nearly three foot curved horns. This brought an amazed, "oh my' from the voice of Tamar as the creatures bounded out of sight into the hilly wilderness. As the group of travelers traveled further south the rugged hills of Judah became more and more prominent. Yellow-stripped green-bodied lizards darted here and there along the side of the dusty trail as the small caravan traveled by their desert burrows. The landscape along the rugged road grew denser with Silver Thistles and Yellow Centaury Thistles along with various varietals of cacti with their sharp thin protruding needles. Tamar said, "What an irony! Such beauty and wonder in such a desolate place."

To take the minds of the travelers off the steep climb through the rugged clefts, Miryam once again assumed her role as the tour guide stating, "All you first time travelers, I want to bring your attention to the three black figures hovering effortlessly over our heads. That would be the desert vultures waiting for their next meal. Then if you would just gaze your eyes slightly below us near the ravine you will see a jackal warding off two stripped hyena's from what appears to be the carcass of a wild camel. In this land you will see both beauty and the beast. Therefore, look to your left and you will see the shaggy bindweed growing among the rocky clefts dotted by the light blue Slender Safflower. Here and there as you allow your eyes to scan the rugged landscape you will see the blue feather-like petals with their lavender centers reaching above the rocks." Then the one and only person paying any attention to her narrative said, "Oh, Miryam (Mary) the desert of wilderness comes alive by sharing with us what your keen eyes see." Miryam replied, "Thank you Tamar. At least the beauty of Yahuah is not going unnoticed or unappreciated. You are such a dear traveling companion for this long and exhausting trip."

Then out of nowhere a giant black thunder cloud began to cast its dark shadow upon the craggy rocks of the treacherous terrain overshadowing the small caravan. The noise coming from the dark phenomenon was more of a hissing deep growl rather than a rolling thunder. A lone grey wolf began to howl a signal of danger and the air began to become thick with the feeling of evil. Even the baby in the womb of Miryam (Mary) began to squirm and wiggle as she clutched her stomach with both hands. The horses, donkeys and camels became very uneasy as their riders and owners had to prod and tug to keep them moving forward up the rugged path. The children began to clutch to their parents with the youngest ones beginning to cry. The men became tense as they clutched their weapons and their eyes darted here and there rapidly to search out this hidden enemy.

Deep inside that giant black thunder cloud were several minions of Satan preparing to attack the caravan with only one mission in mind. The caravan of travelers must not be allowed to reach the evening campground north of the fortified city of Yriychow (Jericho). The black evil minions were working themselves into a feeding frenzy waiting for the Vulture of Death to arrive to signal the attack. The hissing deep growl from the depths of their throats grew louder and more constant as it echoed against the canyon walls. Their long pointed noses with flaring nostrils protruded from their coal black faces set between two glowing red eyes. Their gnashing of sharp needled pointed fangs and deep shrieking voices served as a reminder not to return to the evil cauldron of the dark lord Satan unless the entire caravan of men, women, children and beasts of burden were destroyed. If they failed they would become the next savory meal of the never satisfied Vulture of Death.

A great gust of wind began to whistle through the rugged hills of wilderness as the beating of the giant black wings of the Vulture of Death beat furiously to the scene of its next slaughter. As the wind intensified its' blowing against the small caravan trapped against the rugged trail of lofty sides and gorges, the group of travelers stopped to huddle for protection against the perceived oncoming storm. The pain in the womb of Miryam (Mary) intensified and she yelled out to Yowceph (Joseph), "We must not stop! Keep them going!" Then in unison Miryam and Tamar began to sing the twenty-third *Thillah* (Psalm) as encouragement. Soon the entire caravan was on the move again as they all sang in beautiful harmony and strained to fight with each step to continue through the gusts of wind from the enormous storm of darkness.

"Yahuah is my Shepherd Who tends the flock and grazes it in the pasture and He is my best friend. I will not lack, fail or be of want. In home pastures of sprouting green grass He makes me crouch on all four legs folded under me. To water of peace He guides me. My vitality of breath He returns. He runs with a sparkle to sustain and protect me on the circular tracks of righteousness on account of His Name. When I am walking in the narrow gorge with its lofty sides with the shade of death and the grave I will not be frightened of evil because You are with me. Your walking stick and Your chastening rod they allow me to breath strongly and sigh as I am consoled. You arrange and set in a row and put in order in front of my face a table with a spread out meal in front of my hating adversaries. You anoint my shaking head with rich perfumed olive oil. My goblet is filled to satisfaction. Surely goodness and compassion like a woman cherishing her fetus will run after me all the days of sunset to sunset of my life. I will dwell and remain in the house and family of Yahuah for the length of days."

The sweet music of the travelers pierced the oversized ears of the monkey-like evil minions. The pain was unbearable as they clawed at each other intensifying the deep throated sound roaring from the dark storm cloud. Then a golden eagle began to effortlessly soar between the dark storm cloud and the small caravan below. Its high pitched scream deafened the deep throated sound emitting from within the dark storm cloud. The minions fought with each other in disorder at the sound of the golden eagle and the giant Vulture of Death took its eyes off the caravan and focused upon attacking the soaring golden eagle. As the Vulture of Death extended its long sharp blood-thirsty talons towards the golden eagle, the eagle let out a mighty scream. Then all of a sudden the whirling blades of heaven appeared slashing and knocking the satanic bird off balance sending it tumbling south across the sky back towards the city of Yruwshalaim (Jerusalem) where it had been hovering over the palace of King Herod the Great. Then instantaneously rays of pure sunlight broke up the dark storm cloud as the evil minions scattered fearing for their lives. Why did the dark lord Satan want to destroy this small caravan?

The small caravan of travelers reached their evening destination safely and quickly made camp. They were totally exhausted and not much conversation took place about the events of the day. Even talkative Miryam (Mary) kept silent as she prepared the evening meal and laid down to rest early that evening staying close to Yowceph (Joseph). The stars came out across the evening sky twinkling as if to say, "Sweet dreams weary travelers. You are safe now. We will watch over you tonight so sleep in peace, children of Yahuah." The weary travelers did rest in peace that night as their weary bodies rested from the traumatic events of the long day.

That very same night far to the east in the territory and city of Babel (Babylon-modern Iraq) Master Magi Hammurabi had gathered his faithful night-watchers to peer into the darkened canvas of the night filled with twinkling lights of the evening stars. *Yareach* the moon, *Tsayar the Messenger* (Mercury), *Nogah the Bright* (Venus), and *Shemesh* the sun were still gathered in the shoulder area of the constellation of *Ariy* (Leo the Lion) Yhuwdah (Judah) forming a flattened semi-circle a distance above *Regaleo* (Regulus) the bright king star. The previous night, *Tsadaq the Righteous* (Jupiter) New King had just entered the back feet of the constellation *Ariy* (Leo the Lion) Yhuwdah (Judah) and was traveling in the valley between the two back feet. The five Magi and their five apprentices watched earnestly as *Tsadaq the Righteous* (Jupiter) New King moved out of the valley between the two back feet and into the lower rounded belly region of the great lion.

As soon as *Tsadaq the Rightwous* (Jupiter) New King left the valley of the back feet and began to inch forward in the lower belly region of the constellation of *Ariy* (Leo the Lion) Yhuwdah (Judah) Meyshek the apprentice of Mag Kadashman from Sippar uttered, "See, little Marduk was right *Tsadaq the Righteous* (Jupiter) New King is going to claim the crown of *Yhuwdah,* Judah just like he said. I just knew it! My best friend knew it all along!" Then Mag Nbuwzardan from Opis scolded, "Hush, apprentice! Many things can happen as you will note that *Tsadaq the Righteous* is far away from *Regaleo* (Regulus) the bright scepter star of the king." Apprentice Abed Ngow joined in, "Yeah, Meyshak, you need to quit showing off!" Meyshak retaliated and said, "What do you know about it? I am not the one going to sleep every night-watching like you!" Mag Belsha'tstsar from Nippur jumped in to defend his apprentice Abed Ngow, "Both of you need to spend more time observing Magi code of ethics and less time boyhood squabbling." Mag Zabaia from Erech added, "Meyshak, I appreciate your support of your little friend Marduk but remember his lesson at that time was that Magi do not use the stars to predict the future as a timeline. We use the stars to record history and to the best of our wisdom anticipate an event based upon current data." Master Magi Hammurrabi from Babel continued the teaching, "You see Meyshak and little Marduk and the rest of you apprentices, Magi tell the story of the stars as their journeys cross the dark night sky. We as wise men, can predict the coming of an event but not the timing of the event! Do you understand?"

The five apprentices nodded their heads in agreement and Gungunam from Erech, the oldest apprentice jabbed Meyshak in the side with his sharp elbow. Little seven-year old Marduk whispered to Meyshak, "Thanks for standing up for me but the Magi will never admit that I was right and they were wrong." Then in a louder voice little Marduk belted, "Excuse me honorable Magi of the great country of Babel (Babylon-modern Iraq)! May I speak briefly?" His master Mag Hammurabi scoured and said, "Marduk! Don't push it! The subject is closed!" Mag Kadashman stepped in out of curiosity, "Brother Magi, I would like to hear from young Marduk. I am curious to see if my top student in Hebrew history has learned anything in my class as he constantly daydreams and seems to be bored with my instruction. Perhaps now we can learn whether he truly is my top pupil or if he is getting his good marks by some other gain." Then Mag Hammurabi defensively said of his apprentice, "Now, Mag Kadashman let's not get loosed tongue about little Marduk. Yes he is annoying and never seems to pay attention but one thing I can assure you is that he is not a cheater or a liar!"

Then the little seven-year old voice of Marduk pierced the night air of tension, "Please stop arguing and let me seek your wisdom and counsel on a question that I have concerning tonight's action in the sky by *Tsadaq the Righteous*." Once again in astonishment all five

Magi could not believe the natural diplomacy of this little seven-year old. Mag Nbuwzaradan grunted, "Go ahead little Marduk, speak." Marduk stood as tall as his little frame could stretch and said, "Well, I was just wondering. After watching *Tsadaq the Righteous* (Jupiter) New King move through the valley of the back feet and now slowly traveling through the round belly possibly headed to the valley of the front feet. Well.....I was just wondering if a verse from the Hebrew Holy Writ that Mag Kadashman taught us might apply here? The lesson was from the ancient book of *Thillahim* (Psalms) chapter 24:7-10, **"Lift up oh gate openings your heads. Be lifted up oh door openings of the entrance way to the vanishing point of eternity. Then will come in the King of weighty splendor. Who is this King of weighty splendor? Yahuah strong and powerful like a warrior! Yahuah strong in the battle of warfare! Lift up oh gate openings of the entrance way to the vanishing point of eternity. Then will come in the King of weighty splendor. Who is He this King of weighty splendor? Yahuah of a mass of persons organized for war. He is the King of weighty splendor."** What I was wondering is......could the valley of the back feet and the valley of the front feet in the constellation of *Ariy* (Leo the Lion) Yhuwdah (Judah) represent gate openings? Also, could the back feet where *Tsadaq the Righteous* (Jupiter) New King entered represent kingships of the past and the front feet where the scepter of the bright king star is located represent a final and new type of kingship of the future to the vanishing point of eternity? After all.... there is a possibility that this is the destination of *Tsadaq the Righteous* (Jupiter) New King! I...I...I am just asking."

Mag Nbuwzaradan threw up his hands into the air and replied, "Speculation! Pure speculation and guess work! Apparently young Marduk has not learned his lesson about trying to predict the future by the stars after all! You have a lot of hard work to do Mag

Hammurabi." Then Mag Kadashman jumped into the conversation, "I don't quite agree Mag Nbuwzaradan. Young Marduk did not state that this was going to happen but merely asked if this was a future possibility." Mag Zabaia shook his head in agreement saying, "I agree with Mag Kadashman. Looking at possible events in the future based upon the recorded data of past movements and events is not a violation of the Magi Code of Ethics. Young Marduk has simply questioned a reasonable deduction according to recent events to which he has personally witnessed."

After listening intently and stroking his square cropped beard Master Mag Hammurabi added, "Brother Magi. I have listened to young Marduk and your responses. Yes, young Marduk is my apprentice and it would make me proud to have him come to a correct conclusion in this matter. However, as the Master Magi my personal feelings can't cloud or get in the way of such an important event as this. Therefore, brother Nbuwzaradan I must state that you have allowed your emotions of merely focusing on the obnoxious characteristics of young Marduk to overrule your wisdom in this instance. I must agree with the other Magi that his questions are valid and must be recorded as a possibility for the reason of outcome for the movement of the stars. Now, young Marduk, I must commend you on a substantive intuition and applaud you in the way you presented the question as a possibility and not the ultimate outcome of your observations. One day you will be known among the finest and wisest Magi in Babel (Babylon-modern Iraq) as long as you pursue your dreams with due diligence and hold true to your unwavering convictions based upon correct and accurate information." Then all the Magi including Mag Nbuwzaradan and their apprentices congratulated young Marduk and proceeded down the hill to get some rest before the next evening of night-watching.

11

That very next morning, the fourth day of travel, the travelers were invigorated after a good night's rest. There was a renewed excitement in the camp because today's destination would take them to the outskirts of the small village of *Beyth-aniy*, which means 'house of dates' originating from the old Chaldee (Babylonian) language (Bethany or modern El-Aziriye in the Hebrew language meaning 'Place of Lazarus'). *Beyth-aniy* is located on the eastern slope of *Har HaZeitim* (The Mount of Olives). This is the hill facing the old city of Yruwshalaim (Jerusalem) on the eastern side of Kidron creek. This location for the evening's campsite will put them five miles east of the great city of Yruwshalaim (Jerusalem) just an hour to an hour and a half walking distance from the small village of *Beyth-aniy* (Bethany). After a light breakfast the eager travelers were on the dusty road leading south to the walled city of *Yriychow* (Jericho) and then west to the little village of *Beyth-aniy* (Bethany). The bright and cheerful rays of the early morning sunshine felt good on the faces of the caravan of travelers.

In the city of Yruwshalaim (Jerusalem) the same bright and happy early morning rays of the rising sun shone through the lattice windows of the bedroom of King Herod the Great and were met with the black doom and gloom demonic countenance of the king. He grunted and rambled and raved about each piece of royal clothing that was selected for him to wear by his wardrobe servants. Herod would throw the garments back into the faces of his loyal servants or would toss them wildly about the room leaving the bewildered servants to rapidly return back to the closet to fetch a different set of clothing. The bedroom soon became the scene of disheveled piles of clothing scattered recklessly about the entire room. King Herod being short on patience eventually kicked the trembling servants out of his sight threatening them with their very lives. He muttered to the two guards, "Those worthless buffoons! Don't they know that it is less than forty-eight hours before the celebration of *Chag HaCukkah* (Feast of Tabernacles)? Prince Antipas and I have pressing dinners to host and meetings with important visiting dignitaries to conduct and they want to dress me to look like a court jester! I am their great king and not some stupid fool! Worthless pigs, all of them, just worthless, I should get rid of the whole bunch!"

Outside the palace walls, inside the home of Ya'kov Melek'Beyth Aer (James Henry Ayers) the fan maker, while eating breakfast with his guests Matityahu ben Levi and son *Qatan Yow* (Little Joe), ten-year old Chizqiy Aer (Charles Ayers) asked his father, "*Ab* (father) may I show *Qatan Yow* our city? We have been cooped up here for days now. I want to introduce him to my friends and have some fun." Ya'kov looked up from his plate of fresh fruit and scrambled eggs and said, "What do you think old friend, Matityahu? Shall we release our captive prisoners on grounds of good behavior?" Matityahu ben Levi finished chewing a piece of freshly baked raison bread and replied, "I believe that a reprieve of their tortuous imprisonment for a period of six hours would give both parties peace of mind. However, *Qatan Yow* (Little Joe) needs to be back by high noon because we need to make the final arrangements for the arrival of Yowceph (Joseph) and Miryam (Mary) with the Roman soldiers." Ya'kov Melek'Beyth Aer (James Henry Ayers) said, "Well, that settles it then, reprieve until high noon today....." Before he could finish his sentence both boys bounded up from the reclining table and headed out the front door for a morning loaded with the excitement of adventure.

Ten-year old Chizqiy and eleven-year old *Qatan Yow* bounded down the cobble stone streets of the Upper City of Yruwshalaim (Jerusalem) headed north towards the Palace of Herod. After they had traveled a few blocks the two boys were met by a group of older teenagers. Their ring leader was sixteen-year old Kaiaphas the spoiled son of one of the leading Pharisees. Chizqiy (Charles) slowed to a walk and said to *Qatan Yow* (Little Joe), "Never mind them, they are just friends of the troublemaker Kaiaphas." Then Kaiaphas shouted, "Hey fan-maker boy, who is the rich boy following you like a well-trained puppy dog?" All the older boys laughed and began to taunt the two younger and smaller boys. Chizqiy (Charles) quipped, "He is my friend, so leave us alone! We are not bothering you!" Then two of the older boys grabbed the arms of Chizqiy and held him for Kaiaphas who said, "New boy, do you want to see what happens when you are disrespectful of the son of a Pharisee?" *Qatan Yow* (Little Joe) calmly replied as his friend struggled in the attempt to get free from the vice-like grip of the two older boys, "I would absolutely love to see it but I don't think the mounted patrol of the two Roman soldiers that I hear coming around the corner up the street would be as obliging." The older boys turned their heads and sure enough heard the hoof beats of horses coming from up the street. They threw Chizqiy (Charles) to the ground and quickly ran away. Kaiaphas shouted, "We will meet again fan boy. Next time you and your trained dog won't be so lucky!"

Qatan Yow (Little Joe) helped up his friend and Chizqiy (Charles) questioned, "How did you know they were coming?" *Qatan Yow* answered, "The last two days I have observed them coming down the street on patrol at this very same time. I didn't know exactly where they came from but I did know that they were coming besides you could hear their heavy hoof beats a mile away from carrying that heavy armor." Chizqiy impressed said, "What else have your keen eyes noticed?" *Qatan Yow* pointed towards the blue sky and noted, "The sun is rising and we only have until noon to conclude our adventure, so let's get going!" At that Chizqiy (Charles) led *Qatan Yow* (Little Joe) through the neighborhood on a grand tour of adventure.

The two energetic boys raced as they zig-zagged through the busy morning traffic as everyone seemed in a hurry to make the final preparations for the upcoming *Chag HaCukkah*, the Feast of Tabernacles. After turning the corner at the Palace of Herod and heading east towards the old Hasmonaean Palace. Chizqiy (Charles) quickly darted into a small south alleyway between two large houses belonging to Sadducee *kohen*, (priests). "Where are we going," asked *Qatan Yow* (Little Joe). Chizqiy replied, "Shhh, just keep quiet and follow me!" At the end of the alleyway was an old rickety shed with the sound of young voices coming from behind the half-hanging wooden door. Chizqiy held his finger to his lips signaling for *Qatan Yow* to stop and stand still. Then with a quick jerk on the old wooden door handle Chizqiy roared in a low voice, "*Heach* (aha)! What are you heathen boys doing in here?" Then the inside of the old shed exploded with a ruckus of loud banging and dull thuds as bodies flew against the sides of the old wooden dwelling. "*Oiy vey*, oh pain, *how* (oh) Chizqiy! We thought you were one of those *gowy* (pagan) Roman soldiers on patrol!" exclaimed a small voice from inside.

Then a skinny little curly black haired boy stepped into the doorway and shook the hand of Chizqiy (Charles). The black-haired boy continued, "Where you been champ? We have been missing you?" Chizqiy replied, "Been busy! Never mind that, I want you

129

to meet someone. *Qatan Yow*, Little Joe, this is Kaleb." *Qatan Yow*, Little Joe, acknowledged, "*Shalom!*" and Kaleb returned the greeting, "*Shalom Tav!*" Then curiosity got the best of *Qatan Yow*, "So what ya guys doing in there?" Kaleb replied, "We are playing *kugalach* trying to beat the record of the champ here. He was able to pick up the five wooden dice and all land on the back of his hand eight times in a row last week. Never seen nothin' like it but boy that Chizqiy is good I'm tellin ya! Are you guys here to play?" Chizqiy (Charles) butted in and said, "*Lo*! (No!) We have to get going because we have to be home by noon and I want to show *Qatan Yow*, Little Joe a few more things before everything is busy with *Chag HaCukkah*, the Feast of Tabernacles. You boys stay out of trouble and I will see you next week after the festival." Then after a round of handshakes the two boys went running back up the alley for their next conquest.

Just as they turned the corner at lightning speed of their pre-teen feet to enter the busy street again, Chizqiy (Charles) leading the way suddenly came to an abrupt stop with the impact of running into a stone wall and *Qatan Yow* (Little Joe) crashed into his back. Both boys bounced backwards and fell to the ground dazed and confused. All they could see with blurred vision was a massive figure standing over them with a deep voice saying, "Well what do we have here, a couple of the local Hebrew urchins scouring the streets and who are probably running from the authorities?" They had run smack into the large body guard of a very wealthy businessman who was traveling in the opposite direction towards the palace of King Herod. Their eyes became the size of plates and fear seized their shaking bodies. As two massive hands roughly grabbed the front of both of the boy's tunics and jerked them off the ground suspending them in the air just above the ground, another voice was heard.

"Zeus, we don't have time for this. You have got to get me to the palace of Herod to deliver the important message about the meeting at noon. Since I am not exactly sure where we are going, we don't have precious time to waste! Now drop these alley rats and let's get going." The body guard Zeus obeyed his master and the two boys fell to the ground in a heap. Just as the wealthy merchant and his body guard began to walk away, *Qatan Yow* (Little Joe) spoke up as the boys began to get back upon their feet, "Excuse me sir, we are not alley rats. We are curriers of important messages because we know the streets of Yruwshalaim (Jerusalem) better than anyone." *Chizqiy* (Charles) gave him a sharp elbow in the side with a puzzled yet stern look on his face. *Qatan Yow* (Little Joe) paid him no attention and continued speaking, "My partner and I are the fastest and best in the city. As a matter of fact sir, just before our unfortunate and apologetic collision with Zeus here, we were on our way from completing an important task. I know very well the meeting at the palace that you are speaking of since I am required to be in attendance myself. My name is *Qatan Yow* (Little Joe) and my partner is *Chizqiy* (Charles). My master has a personal invitation to represent the trading delegation of Rome."

This got the attention of the wealthy merchant as he replied, "Well Zeus, it looks like good fortune has run into us at last. *Qatan Yow* my name is Maqus from the country of Helene (Greece) and I also am to represent the trading delegation of Rome. Since I need to find and make final arrangements for evening accommodations, I might just be interested in your services. I will pay you and your partner a drachma (16 cents) each to deliver a message for me." *Qatan Yow* questioned, "I thought you told Zeus that the message was of great importance. We are not stupid alley rats, we are young businessmen like yourself and we have others waiting for our services. Come on Chizqiy let's go!" Then *Qatan Yow* grabbed Chizqiy (Charles) by the arm and began to walk off. Maqus immediately spoke up, "Wait let's not be hasty. So what does one usually have to pay for your services?" *Qatan Yow* stopped and replied, "Well sir, since our clients are only royalty and businessmen like yourself, we normally get a Roman *aureus* (4 dollars) each which is twenty-five Helene (Greek) drachma each. However, since by our misfortune we have caused you much delay, this time and this time only we would settle for four Roman *denarii* each (64 cents) which would be a Helene (Greek) *stater* each."

Maqus the Helene (Greek) businessman agreed, "Ok, fine you have a deal. Since you will be at the meeting, I will pay you then." *Qatan Yow* shook his head in disagreement and replied, "Lo! (No)! You must pay my partner the drachma (16 cents) that you originally offered and I will collect the rest at the meeting." Maqus stunned said, "You are a smart businessman. Fine, Zeus pay the boy!" As Zeus reached into his money belt and gave Chizqiy the drachma (16 cents) *Qatan Yow* (Little Joe) continued, "We are not fools. It is the custom of two business men to exchange a security deposit until the deal is completed. We will return the drachma (16 cents) to you and you must give us a small token of promise such as that golden bracelet on the wrist of Zeus." Maqus stroked his beard and grumbled, "Well I never in my life have met a kid who knows his business. Zeus give him your bracelet and let's quit wasting our time here." Zeus complied with the request of his master and handed the golden bracelet to *Qatan Yow* and then took back the drachma (16 cents) from Chizqiy. Then Maqus handed a small scroll containing a message for the palace to *Qatan Yow* (Little Joe) which he tucked safely inside his tunic belt. Just before the two parties departed their own ways, *Qatan Yow* (Little Joe) had the last word, "I will be at the front of the palace at 11:45 to complete our transaction. If you don't show or are late I will keep the golden bracelet and King Herod will have your head." Then the two boys turned on their heels and ran as fast as they could toward the palace. Chizqiy had a hard time keeping up because his asthma began to kick in with all the excitement. Therefore, *Qatan Yow* slowed to a brisk walk allowing Chizqiy to catch his breath and lead the way to the palace muttering all the way, "I can't believe you did this. What were you thinking? We are going to be in so much trouble when we get home. I just know a stick is waiting for my backside when my *ab* (father) gets wind of this. I can't believe that I kept quiet and let you do this."

Time passed quickly as Chizqiy led *Qatan Yow* through many shortcuts avoiding the bustle of the heavy street traffic. They had finally reached their destination standing in front of the Palace of King Herod the Great on the southeast corner of the Upper City of Yruwshalaim (Jerusalem). Their little hearts were pounding rapidly in their chests with great excitement and a touch of fear as they stood in front of the palace of one of the most ruthless kings in the world. Now all they had to do was deliver the scroll containing the message bearing the seal of Maqus and addressed to the king himself. *Qatan Yow* (Little Joe) silently handed the scroll to one of the front guards who when he saw the seal and to whom it was addressed quickly turned and headed inside the doors of the outer wall. The boys quickly beat a hasty retreat and headed back south to the home of the father of Chizqiy, the famous fan maker. The seriousness of the matter quickly wore off as they slapped each other on the back and giggled as they skipped and playfully ran all the way back home with Chizqiy stopping only a couple of times briefly to catch his breath as they chattered non-stop reliving their morning adventure in astonishment.

After arriving back to the home of the *ab* (father) of Chizqiy, *Qatan Yow* quickly changed into some of his finest clothing so that he could accompany his *ab* (father) Matityahu ben Levi to the business lunch hosted by King Herod the Great. Soon they were being carried in a fancy litter that Matityahu ben Levi had hired for the festive occasion after their arrival in Yruwshalaim (Jerusalem). After they arrived at the palace a little early, *Qatan Yow* begged his *ab* (father) if he could remain outside the palace wall for a short time to watch the parade of fine litters and important dignitaries arriving. Matityahu ben Levi slipped one of the guards a few coins to keep an eye on his son and then went inside. Shortly after that, a litter decked out in gold drapes, large ostrich feathers, small tinkling bells, and large brass post caps arrived that caught the attention of young *Qatan Yow*. Leading the way of this beautiful litter was Zeus, which meant that Maqus was inside and *Qatan Yow* was about to have money in his belt. The litter was lowered and Maqus, the wealthy Helene (Greek) merchant stepped out from inside. Zeus immediately stood beside him and they began to walk to the entrance of the palace wall.

Qatan Yow, carefully approached the formidable businessman and his massive body guard and lowering his head and holding out the golden bracelet said, "*Shalom*, excuse me master Maqus, I believe this golden bracelet belongs to your servant Zeus." Maqus stopped, looked at the golden bracelet and then back to the young boy and replied, "Is that you *Qatan Yow?* I did not recognize you all dressed up. Is all well?" *Qatan Yow* answered, "All is well. King Herod the Great awaits your arrival." Then Maqus nodded to Zeus who placed two Helene (Greek) *stater,* worth sixty-four cents each, into the palm of his hand and then took the golden bracelet from him. Maqus and Zeus continued and entered behind the palace wall while *Qatan Yow*, who was smiling from ear to ear lingered a brief while longer.

Inside, Maqus met Matityahu ben Levi who was standing just a short distance from the wall gate. After greetings and gripping each other's elbow, Matityahu ben Levi said, "I am glad I caught up with you before we go inside. I am waiting for my son who will be joining us shortly but I wanted to ask you if you reviewed my offer of the mining expedition that you requested of me." Maqus cleared his throat and said, "Yes, I did and I found it twice as high as any of your competitors. I must decline your offer because I can't make a profit under your proposal. Besides, there is rumor that you can no longer afford to live at the Estates in Arimathea and have moved to the remote village of Nazareth." Matityahu ben Levi responded as *Qatan Yow* (Little Joe) joined his side, "First of all Maqus, when does a wise businessman make decisions based upon rumor instead of fact. Second, I would like you to meet my son, Yowceph (Joseph) of Arimathea."

A stunned Maqus stammered, "*Qatan Yow*, is your son? But...." Matityahu ben Levi being surprised interrupted and said, "How did you know the family nickname of my son?" Maqus quickly stated as he was backing up towards the palace entrance in retreat as he remembered the last time he negotiated with someone from the Estates of Arimathea it cost him four times as much as the original offer, "Very, wise Matityahu ben Levi to send your son out to scout my negotiating strategies, I accept your original offer for the mining proposal and will sign the contract after lunch. I don't want any part of negotiations with you. See you after lunch!" A befuddled Matityahu ben Levi looked down at his son, *Qatan Yow* (Little Joe) who shrugged his shoulders playing innocent. Then Little Joe said, "Come on *ab* (father) I am starved and my stomach is grumbling in protest of a lack of fine food. You know that we must not keep the king waiting." Matityahu ben Levi stroked his beard and shook his head in bewilderment asking himself silently, "*What on earth just happened?*"

135

Back on the dusty road northeast of the great city of Yruwshalaim (Jerusalem) a weary but excited caravan of travelers reached the outskirts of the little village of *Beyth-aniy* (Bethany) located on the eastern slope of *Har HaZeitim* (The Mount of Olives) just before sunset. Now they are just less than a two hour journey to the great city. Miryam (Mary) and Tamar the wife of Nathan ben Yow'ash went to the local watering well to gather water for the evening meal preparation. At the well they met a local woman named Aziel with her two young daughters two-year old Martha and six-month old Miryam (Mary). Miryam shared with Aziel that she and Tamar had traveled clear from the little village of Nazareth to attend the upcoming *Chag HaCukkah*, the Feast of Tabernacles at sundown on the next day. Then Aziel revealed that her husband owned an olive and a palm-date grove. Miryam said to Aziel, "Oh my, my mouth is just watering for fresh date cakes." Aziel replied, "You two just stay right here and watch my girls and I will return with fresh dates for your evening meal." Tamar responded, "No, we couldn't ask you to do that." Aziel shook her head and said, "Oh yes you can. From the looks of Miryam she needs good food for nourishment. We have an overabundance and you can call it good hospitality from the welcoming party." Then Aziel sat Martha on the lap of Tamar and Miryam (Mary) held infant Miryam as Aziel disappeared in the distance with her clay jar full of water.

Tamar said to Miryam, "Aziel is so nice, we must get her a gift from the market and present it to her on our way back home." Miryam (Mary) agreed, "Yes, Tamar that would be great. Oh, how I can't wait to hold the child in my womb and look into his eyes like I am hers." Tamar was quick to question, "How do you know it is a boy?" Miryam blushed at her slip of the tongue and said, "All the village women including the midwife have said that as low as

I am carrying this child it has to be a boy. Also, the baby is very rambunctious and requires all my attention just like the big baby I am married too." Then both women bust out in laughter causing little Martha to giggle. Not much time had passed when in a distance they could see Aziel leading a donkey with a couple of small bulging sacks bobbing up and down one on each side of the animal. When Aziel arrived at the watering well she said, "Sorry it took longer than I had anticipated but I couldn't get old Bil'am (Balaam) pulled away from his night feeding. He is such a stubborn animal. Were the girls good? I see you were laughing when I came upon you." Tamar quickly said, "The girls were perfect *mal'akiym* (angels) and we were laughing at our stubborn donkey husbands and their night feedings." Then all three women burst out into laughter once again and made light chit-chat as they talked about their families and how a woman's work is never done.

    Aziel handed the reigns of Bil'am to Miryam as Miryam handed infant Miryam to her mother, Aziel. Then Miryam said, "Aziel it was so good of you to meet us strangers with such hospitable favor. However, we better get our jars of water and head back to camp before our husbands start baying for their supper." Aziel giggled and replied, *"Ken* (yes) you are right the sun will be set soon and they will be expecting you. Now I brought each of you a bag of dates and Miryam I want you to use Bil'am for transportation on the rest of your journey. Someone in your condition has no business trying to maneuver the crowed streets of the capital city Yruwshalaim (Jerusalem)." "Oh, I can't ask you to do that," Miryam protested. Aziel responded, "You didn't ask and you will listen to me. Think about the safety of your child. You can drop old Bil'am off here on your way back home after the festival and that is the last I will hear of it." All three women said their good-byes and gave each other a hug. Aziel and little Martha waved good-bye as Miryam and Tamar headed back to camp.

When they reached the camp, Miryam (Mary) and Tamar shared with Yowceph (Joseph) and Nathan ben Yow'ash about how they met Aziel at the watering well and how the conversation turned to dates and then Aziel returned with the donkey. However, the men soon lost interest in the story and began discussing the next day's travel agenda as Nathan ben Yow'ash and Tamar would stop in Yruwshalaim (Jerusalem) to register and how Yowceph (Joseph) and Miryam (Mary) would continue on to Beth-Lechem (Bethlehem) meaning the 'house of bread' to register as descendants of the bloodline of ancient King David. After an evening meal of their remaining traveling rations and fresh date cakes, the travelers laid back next to the glowing campfire and admired the twinkling stars overhead. Tonight the stars seemed to be more active and twinkled repeatedly as if telling a secret bedtime story. Soon the campfire conversations grew silent as they all drifted off to sleep.

As the caravan of travelers were settling down for their last evening of camping under the stars, further east of their campsite in the country of Babel (Babylon, modern Iraq) the magi and their apprentices were just arriving at their usual night-watching location. Master Mag Hammurabi addressed his fellow magi and their apprentices, "Brother Magi and young apprentices, the night-watching of last evening could have been the beginning of the fulfillment of our devoted efforts of recording the story of the stars. As you look up into the blinking heavens above, you can observe *Yareach* the moon, *Tsayar the Messenger* (Mercury), *Nogah the Bright* (Venus), and *Shemesh* the sun are still gathered in the shoulder area of the constellation of *Ariy* (Leo the Lion) Yhuwdah (Judah) forming a flattened semi-circle a distance above *Regaleo* (Regulus) the bright king star. *Tsadaq the Righteous* (Jupiter) New King is still traveling over the rounded belly of *Ariy* (Leo the Lion)."

"My young apprentice, seven year old Marduk made an astounding observation last evening and presented a very valid question to the group of Magi. After careful review of all the data from the charts as well as the detailed documented notes, we the leading Magi of the country of Babel (Babylon, modern Iraq) have concluded that tonight could possibly lead to the announcement of a New King in the country of *Yhuwdah* (Judah). It is very critical tonight that each of us watch diligently each and every twinkle of *Tsadaq the Righteous* (Jupiter) New King. Nothing should be left unobserved including the smallest movement. Therefore, as Master Magi, I have decided that the five Magi along with young apprentices Marduk and Meyshak will watch only *Tsadaq the Righteous* (Jupiter) New King and apprentices Shadrak and Abed Ngow will observe the group of stars in the semi-circle above *Regaleo* (Regulus). This will leave apprentice Gungunam to observe any movement in *Regaleo* (Regulus) itself. Does everyone understand their assignment for this evening's night-watching?" All responded, "Yes, Master Hammurabi." Then the tedious night-watching began with eyes straining into the vast dark canvas dotted with multitudes of twinkling bright stars of white light.

The evening of night-watching progressed into the very late hours of the night and *Tsadaq the Righteous* (Jupiter) New King rounded the top of the belly of the constellation of *Ariy* (Leo the Lion) Yhuwdah (Judah) and then headed straight to the valley between the front two legs. There it remained in the valley of the front two legs and continued on the path straight to *Regaleo* (Regulus) the bright king star between the front two feet of *Ariy* (Leo the Lion) Yhuwdah (Judah). As the evening stars began to fade and the morning light began to blossom Master Magi Hammurabi stood behind his seven year old apprentice Marduk and placed both hands on his shoulders and said, "I am very proud of my young apprentice. It appears that he possesses a very rare wisdom of insight into night-watching. We may owe this young man our deepest apologies for doubting his new found gift." When Mag Hammurabi made this statement apprentices Marduk and Meyshak grinned from ear to ear and their eyes beamed with that 'I told you so' look. Then Mag Hammurabi continued, "Today, before we lay down to rest I want each of us to get packed for a possible journey to the capital city Yruwshalaim (Jerusalem) of the country of Yhuwdah (Judah). It is in my wisest judgment that tonight we will know if a New King has been announced in that great county. Let's go home, we have a lot of work to get done." As the group of night-watchers made their way down the hill towards the house, the two young apprentices locked arm in arm and skipped all the way in front of the weary-eyed group. The joyous unspoken words of these two apprentices could be seen in the playful travel back to the headquarters of their apologetic magi masters.

12

Yowceph (Joseph) and Miryam (Mary) were awakened during the next morning's pre-dawn darkness as Bil'am the donkey wanted his morning feed. What began as a soft occasional baying escalated into a high pitched repeated request for his breakfast. His demands for a morning meal soon disturbed the rest of the animals whose voices added to the slumber-disturbing chaos. It was hard to tell if the other animals were requesting Bil'am to go back to sleep or were joining in the noise in full agreement of his early morning request. Whatever the reason for such a ruckus did not matter because the chorus of non-stop baying soon got the attention of their human masters in the camp who were not too happy to get up so early. However, since it was the last day of travel and a short day's journey to the traveler's destination of the great city Yruwshalaim (Jerusalem) the entire camp was cheerful as their opening eyes met the sliver of light beginning to dimly peek from the east into the last lingering darkness of the previous night. The obnoxious baying of hungry animals was soon replaced with humming and melodious singing throughout the entire camp praising Yahuah for such a glorious day.

Yowceph (Joseph) and Miryam (Mary) ate a quick breakfast against the backdrop of the hues of yellowish-oranges mixed with pinks of the early morning sky. The morning air was fresh and crisp and was filled with the melodious chirping from the birds in the hills of Yhuwdah (Judah). Then the entire camp was all abuzz with activity of final packing and putting out the lingering campfires.

One by one they began to mount their animals or load their camping supplies upon their shoulders and began to journey west to the great city of Yruwshalaim (Jerusalem). Yowceph helped Miryam get settled on the back of Bil'am and joined their traveling companions from Nazareth Tamar and her husband Nathan ben Yow'ash on the dusty trail leading to their final destination.

They had not traveled even one hundred yards when Miryam (Mary) exploded with singing of one of ancient King David's Thillahyim (Psalms) number fifteen, *"A poem set to notes for instrumental music by David. Oh Yahuah who will turn aside from the road for lodging as a sojourning guest in Your tent? Who will stay permanently on Your sacred mountain? He who walks entirely in the integrity of truth and practices righteousness and speaks an arrangement of words of the truth in his heart of feelings and intellect. He does not slander with his tongue and he does not do evil to his friend Disgrace he does not lift up against his neighbor. In his eyes the spurned has been disesteemed but those who revere Yahuah he honors. He has sworn an oath seven times as a declaration to be made good for nothing and will not change it. He did not give his silver at interest on a loan. A donation against the innocent has not taken. He who does these things will not be shaken to the vanishing point of eternity."* It did not take long for the whole caravan to join in the joyful singing as their beautiful blended voices echoed in the hills cascading towards the great city Yruwshalaim (Jerusalem) over the sacred mountain ahead of the caravan seeming to announce their arrival to Yahuah's tent for the great celebration of *Chag HaCukkah*, the Feast of Tabernacles at sundown today.

After an hour's travel, there in the short distance were the massive walls of the great city Yruwshalaim (Jerusalem) towering towards the heavens. The pure white upper porches of the Temple could be seen peeking over the top of the eastern wall. As they ascended upon *Har HaZeitim* (Mount of Olives) Yowceph (Joseph) looked back at Miryam (Mary) and quoted from the second chapter of *Thillahyim* (Psalms) **2:6-7, "But I have anointed My king on My sacred Mountain Tsiyiown (Zion) of the city of Yruwshalaim (Jerusalem). I will recount of the appointed enactment of Yahuah. He said to Me, "You are My Son. Today I have born You to show lineage!"** Miryam smiled at Yowceph and said, "Someday when we return but not today!" Then she gently patted her protruding belly and said to Yowceph so that no one else could hear, "We have plenty of time before the prophecy of our ancestor King David is fulfilled."

Then the travelers descended down *Har HaZeitim* (Mount of Olives) the Holy Mountain of Yahuah and headed northwest towards *Gath-Shemen*, meaning 'press of olives', (Garden of Gethsemane). The path was wedged in between stands of brown, gnarly barked trees covered with silver-white leaves like an opened umbrella. The shaded forest floor was dotted with patches of small red poppies and an occasional bush of bright pink begonias. Miryam (Mary) could also see deep under the trees trumpet vines loaded with its bright red trumpet flowers with pink bell tips. Almost going unnoticed were the small patches of light lavender petunias with their deep violet centers. Miryam inhaled a deep breath of the aromatic scents of the garden air. Just as she was beginning to exhale all of a sudden she felt an uncanny sense of deep prayer and betrayal. She could not explain it but the infant seemed to cling to the walls of her womb with deep reservation.

Then out loud in a quiet voice she began to recite the fifth chapter of Thillahyim (Psalms), *"To the superintendent of music on stringed instruments a poem set to music. A poem set to notes of instrumental music by David. What I say broaden out Your ears with Your hand*

and listen to oh Yahuah and understand my murmuring complaint. Prick up Your ears and hearken to the sound of the voice of my cry for help my King and My Yah because to You I will intercede in prayer. Yahuah in the morning at dawn the break of day I will arrange myself to You and I will lean forward and peer into the distance to observe and wait. Because You are not a Yah pleased with morally wrong. You will not turn aside from the road to lodge as a sojourning guest with evil. Those who boast will not place themselves in front of Your eyes. You hate all who practice perverse evil. You will destroy the ones speaking an arrangement of words of deceiving lies. The man of blood and wicked vanity Yahuah will loathe and detest."

"But I in the abundance of Your kindness, I will go into Your house and I will prostrate in homage towards Your sacred temple in reverence towards You. Oh Yahuah! Guide me in Your righteousness because of my hating adversaries. Make Your trodden road as a course of life straight and even in front of me. Because there does not exist in their mouth faithfulness. Their center part is the desire for ruin and their throat is an open grave sepulcher. With their tongue they speak smooth. Hold them guilty oh Yahuah. Let them fall from their own purpose. In the army of their quarrelling and breaking away from Your just authority misleads them and pushes them away into transgressions. Because they have quarreled and broke away from Your just authority. But let be gleeful all fleeing for protection and confiding in You. To the vanishing point of eternity they will shout with joy because You will cover and protect them. They will be gleeful in You those having affection for Your Name. Because You will bless the righteous oh Yahuah. You will encircle him with a large shield with kindness."

Just as they left the garden they came to a fork in the road. One fork leading directly east five hundred feet was the farthest northern gate on the eastern wall called *tso'n sha'ar* (sheep gate). This gate led to the pens where the flocks of sheep were kept for temple sacrifice. Since this was about a half a day from a major feast the bleating of sheep could be heard from behind the wall. The baby in the womb of Miryam (Mary) squirmed as if it knew the fate of the sacrificial sheep crying behind the wall. However, they would not take this fork but instead followed the other fork leading northwest about another fifteen hundred feet to the corner of the northern city wall. The path was now packed with traffic going in both directions. As Yowceph (Joseph) continued to lead obedient Bil'am bearing the burden of Miryam and unborn child, he turned and smiled at Miryam (Mary) with excitement written all over his face. Miryam returned the smile and nodded in agreement.

As they turned the corner, streams of people could be seen for miles coming from the north trying to enter into the northern gates of the great walled city of Yruwshalaim (Jerusalem). Miryam (Mary) quickly thought about these people and their journey from their homes to take part in the feast and the Roman Census. Various languages and dialects could be detected as the overflowing roadways swelled with animals and people. Tamar, who had been walking beside Miryam shouted over the noise, "It looks like this is where I better say good-bye Miryam because of the noise and crowds. I don't think I will have a chance once we get inside. I will see you after the feast and we will journey back home together." Miryam reached out to grab her hand and said, "We will not be long in Beyth Lechem (Bethlehem) and should be back in Yruwshalaim (Jerusalem) before sunset. It will be great to see grandfather and Qatan Yow (Little Joe) again. Thanks for the company and we will meet you at this gate in eight days." Then she gently kissed the hand of Tamar as they were approaching the middle gate of the Northern Wall which opened up into the Bezetha District. Soon the traffic seemed to crawl to a standstill as the streams of travelers jammed shoulder to shoulder squeezed through the massive wooded gates.

As Yowceph (Joseph) led Bil'am the donkey and Miryam (Mary) through the wooden gates, you could see the Temple on the highest hill far above the sprawling city of the lower Bezetha District. At such a glorious and beautiful sight Miryam burst into reciting the one hundredth chapter of *Thillahyim* (Psalms), **"A poem set to notes for instrument music of extending the hands with a choir of worshippers. Shout for joy that splits the ears to Yahuah all the firm earth. Serve Yahuah with glee. Come in front of His face with shouts of joy. Know that Yahuah is Yah. He has made us and we not ourselves. We are His people and the sheep of His home pasture. Enter into His gate openings with laudation of hymns and into His yard surrounded with walls with extended hands of adoration with a choir of worshippers. Extend your hands in worship and bless His Name. Because Yahuah is good and His kindness is to the vanishing point of eternity. Unto generation to generation of revolution of age is His faithfulness."** Yowceph responded, "*Halal Yah!* (Celebrate to shine the light of Yahuah)"

Those riding on animals had the definite advantage as those on foot gave way to the camels, horses and donkeys. Miryam had a good advantage of being able to see over the heads of all the people and guided Yowceph (Joseph) on which way to go through the crowd and maze of venders hocking their precious wares. Miryam was so thankful to Yahuah for providing Bil'am the donkey for her through the obedience of Ariel. She just could not imagine trying to get through this impatient crowd on foot with her belly sticking out so far. They would have to travel through the entire Bezetha District to get to the west side in order to meet her grandfather Matityahu ben Levi and little Uncle *Qatan Yow* (Little Joe) at the Gennath Gate, which was the entrance into the Upper City. Plans were to meet them just before the high sun (noon) briefly before they traveled on south to Beyth Lechem (Bethlehem) to get registered for the Roman Census and then be back to the Gennath Gate before sunset, the hour that *Chag HaCukkah* (Feast of Tabernacles) would begin. After two hours of pushing, weaving, being pushed and crowded she could see Matityahu ben Levi in the short distance now and shouted, "Grandfather! Grandfather! *Shalom!*" Yowceph could not yet see Matityahu ben Levi because of the tight crowd but he could hear his voice respond, "Miryam! Shalom! Over here!" Yowceph (Joseph) let his ears be his guide until he could see Matityahu ben Levi grinning from ear to ear through his gray beard and *Qatan Yow* (Little Joe) waving his arms as if swatting at swarms of pesky gnats or irritating flies.

Qatan Yow took the lead rope from Yowceph asking a million questions about Bil'am the donkey and the journey. Then Yowceph helped Miryam down from the back of Bil'am as she proceeded to exchange greetings with her grandfather, Matityahu ben Levi. After the brief reunion, Matityahu ben Levi stated, "Reports are that all the villages surrounding Yruwshalaim (Jerusalem) are crammed to overflowing just as bad as the chaos of this city. You two had better get on the road to see if you can beat the swell of people headed to Beyth Lechem (Bethlehem) to get registered for the Roman Census. I will be right here in this same spot just before sundown expecting you. Yowceph, if for some reason that I don't make it here before sundown, here are your passes into the gate for the Upper City. Miryam knows where the fan maker lives." Yowceph nodded and then Matityahu ben Levi handed Yowceph (Joseph) two small brass tickets with a special inscription on both sides. One side was written in Latin *"Invado Unus Gloria Rex"* and the other in Hebrew *"Bow HaKabad HaMelek"*. Both sides meaning, "Enter into the glory of the king." Yowceph quickly secured them in his money belt for safe keeping. They quickly said their good-byes and Yowceph lifted Miryam onto the back of Bil'am and then they were off.

They soon passed the large Pool of Amygdalon and then out the center west gate which was below the towering Palace of Herod. This was the same gate where centuries earlier an aging *kohen* priest Matityahu ben Yowchanan (John) Maccabim and his sons had entered that subsequently began the dynasty of the bloodline of Miryam that King Herod detested with such relentless hatred and burning murderous passion.

The young couple took the southern fork leading five miles south to the little village of Beyth Lechem (Bethlehem) the birthplace of their ancestor King David. This is where they were required by law to register with the Roman Government for the Census. There were many others on the road ahead of them but when Miryam looked back there seemed to be a larger throng following behind them headed in the same direction for the same purpose. It looked like a long trail of ants heading back to the ant hill. About a half a mile from the village of Beyth Lechem (Bethlehem) the flow of traffic in front of Yowceph (Joseph) and Miryam (Mary) ground to a slow and complete stop. Nothing moved and the utterance of complaints could be heard.

As Miryam looked back over her shoulder the stopped stream of traffic behind them seemed to grow further and further to the north. Inch by painstaking inch the line would slowly creep forward and then come once again to a complete standstill. Every now and then Yowceph (Joseph) would hand Miryam (Mary) the water skin to wet her parched throat from the dust and afternoon sun. Bil'am the donkey would shut his eyes and seem to catch a nap between the small incremental spurts of moving forward. Yowceph and Miryam made small talk with the travelers around them to help time go by faster as the sun continued on its set path across the western sky. After much delay they finally reached the entrance of the village where they received instructions on where to go to register for the Roman Census. Moneychangers were present to exchange money with the correct currency at a dishonest exchange rate with Roman military guards in their company for protection.

Patience was running thin and shouting and arguing could be heard in the line in front of them which brought on the scene mounted Roman soldiers. Their presence quickly quieted down the crowd as the Roman Government was not going to tolerate any sign of trouble or objection to this mandated decree from Augustus. The subjects of Rome would willingly be compliant or suffer severe consequences for disobedience. Due to the non-movement of the line, Miryam requested to be let down from Bil'am so that she could stretch her legs. She could not walk very far but at least she could walk on the ground of the birthplace of her ancestor King David.

As Yowceph (Joseph) and Miryam (Mary) talked about their ancestor King David. They visited about him being a shepherd, a brave warrior, a loyal servant to King Sha'uwl (Saul) and finally a mighty king of the nation of Yisra'Yah (Israel). They talked about how in each stage of the life of King David how much he revered and loved Yahuah with every beat of his heart. When even in uncertain times of distress or danger, David knew where his strength came from. Then Yowceph (Joseph) and Miryam (Mary) sang in perfect harmony the one hundred and twenty-first chapter of *Thillahyim* **"*A song to sing with the strolling minstrels of elevated acts. I will raise up my eyes to the range of hills. From where will come my aid? My*** *aid comes from Yahuah, the Maker of the lofty sky where the clouds move and the firm earth. He will not give to fall your foot. He who puts a hedge of thorns about to guard and protect you will not slumber in drowsiness. Lo! He who puts a hedge of thorns about to guard and protect the nation of Yisra'Yah will not slumber in drowsiness or sleep. Yahuah is your hedge of thorns to guard and protect you. Yahuah is your shade on your right hand. The brilliant sun by day of sunset to sunset will not strike you severely or the moon by night as it twists away from the light. Yahuah will put a hedge of thorns about to guard and protect you from all evil. He will put a hedge of thorns about to guard your vitality of breath. Yahuah will put a hedge of thorns about to guard and protect your going out and coming in. From at this time and until the vanishing point of eternity."*

Before they knew it even though it was late afternoon, they were next in line at the registration table which was only taking five people at a time. Yowceph (Joseph) held on to Miryam (Mary) with one hand and with the other hand a tight hold on the lead rope of Bil'am the donkey who didn't seem to mind at all this slow pace and having to stand around doing absolutely nothing. Yowceph listened carefully to the questions being asked by the recorders so that he could speed up the registration process and they could be on their way back to the great city of Yruwshalaim (Jerusalem) before sunset and the beginning of *Chag HaCukkah* (Feast of Tabernacles). The family in front of them finished and turned around exchanging places with Yowceph and Miryam. As the young couple stepped up to the registration table they were met with a demanding voice, "State your name and where you are from." Yowceph (Joseph) answered all the questions all the while the man behind the table never looked up once from his parchment and quill and ink concentrating on his dull and repetitious task at hand.

It was now very late in the afternoon and almost evening as Yowceph was finishing up registering and paying his tax. The contractions of the tightening of the muscles in the womb of Miryam began and were so mild that she didn't even know what was going on. Yowceph lifted Miryam onto the back of Bil'am the donkey and glanced at the sitting sun. He looked up at her and said, "I am glad that is over now we must hurry to Yruwshalaim (Jerusalem) before sundown." Miryam smiled and said, "Yes, I will be so glad to lie down on a comfortable bed tonight at the home of the fan maker. I don't mean to complain but my back has reached its limit of tolerance." As they began to fight their way back through the remaining crowd, Miryam felt a warm liquid beginning to flow under her. She immediately said, "Yowceph (Joseph) we are not going to make it to Yruwshalaim tonight. Stop and find us a place to stay here in Beyth Lechem (Bethlehem)." Yowceph looked back with confidence and replied, "Oh don't worry my little dove. I will have you in your comfortable nest before you know it. We still have a couple of hours before sunset and *Chag HaCukkah* (Feast of Tabernacles)." Miryam looked back with her deep brown eyes and said, "No, Yowceph (Joseph) we won't. I think my water just broke so we must find a place here. Now!" Yowceph stopped Bil'am the donkey dead in his tracks and with panic in his voice replied, "Are you sure? You said it was not time yet. We are supposed to make it back to Nazareth." Miryam remained calm and said in a loving voice, "I know dear but Yahuah must have other plans. Look at the crowd around you. They all will not get registered today and will need a place to stay tonight so we must hurry before they close the Census books for the day." Yowceph (Joseph) tugged on the lead rope and said, "Come on old Bil'am we must hurry no time to be stubborn now." Bil'am obeyed and the search began.

Yowceph began to ask passerby's where the nearest inn was and upon receiving directions traveled with haste to seek accommodations for his laboring wife. Inn after inn was already booked and did not have any rooms to rent. He even offered more money but to no avail. After an hour and a half searching and being told "no room" the sun was sitting in the west. Now the contractions were getting closer together and the pain was intensifying for Miryam as the womb muscles began to push the baby to be delivered. Now the contractions were getting serious and Miryam had a hard time catching her breath because of the pain. Yowceph could see the pain on her face and apologetically said, "I am sorry dear but I am trying the best I can!" Miryam tried to assure him and replied, "I know Yowceph. I am fine just keep moving and trying to find a place."

The pain would stop between contractions and Miryam would catch her breath. Then the pain would begin to intensify as it would build to a climax of a breathtaking level before it would subside. It was now getting dark after hours of searching door to door. Yowceph (Joseph) was in a panic state at this moment and he stopped at a common looking small inn built on a hill with its shingle reading *Chadash Re'Shiyth* meaning, "New Beginnings" or "Fresh Firstfruit". He beat loudly on the wooden door and a short balding man opened the door and said, "*Shalom ger!* (Welcome guest!)" Yowceph replied, "Please sir, my wife is about to give birth to a child and we need to rent a room right away! I will pay with all I have in my possession!" The balding man answered, "My name is Ger'shom (Gereshom) but we have no rooms left." Yowceph determined not to be denied one more time responded, "We will take a small back storage room or anywhere for my wife to give birth." Ger'shom stuck out his lower lip and said, "*Lo!* (No)! I can't afford to have that kind of ruckus going on in the earshot of my other guests. You must move on and find somewhere else. Sorry I can't help you." As the innkeeper was closing the door in Yowceph's face, Yowceph (Joseph) said, "Sir, as Yahuah lives can you swear an oath that you don't own an inch of property where we can seek shelter for the night so that my wife can deliver our baby?" The innkeeper Ger'shom looked Yowceph in the eyes and answered, "I give an oath to Yahuah our Yah that I do not have any more rooms or any living space. Just the barn behind the house is left and you wouldn't want that!" Yowceph's eyes grew big and blurted out in an excited voice, "We will take it! How much?" The puzzled innkeeper looked back at Yowceph and said, "You do? Well then, nothing! Just go and see me in the morning before you leave. I must attend to my guests who are waiting for their meal!"

When Yowceph (Joseph) returned to Miryam (Mary) and Bil'am the donkey, she was trying to fight off another contraction. She was bent over clutching her stomach trying to breathe through the intense and torturous pain. After the contraction subsided Yowceph mopped her sweating forehead with the sleeve of his cloak and said, "I found a place to stay! It's not much but at least it is something." Then he led Miryam and Bil'am the donkey down and around to the back of the inn to the entrance of the barn. He helped Miryam (Mary) dismount from Bil'am and grabbed the oil lamp for light. After the small lantern was lit they entered the front of the barn being careful to shut the crude fence gate made of branches and rope behind them.

The barn was a small cave hewn by hand out of the side of the hill. It was dark and musty and smelled of animal dung. As they surveyed the area they were met with glowing eyes of about a dozen chickens who had roosted for the night in one of the corners. Not too far from the chickens was a nanny goat with her legs folded under her and chewing her cud. At the far back of the cave appeared to be a small crude manger hewn into the solid rock. Just below the manger lying down was a very curious donkey staring into the light of the lantern with its ears erect wondering what was this intrusion into the night life of barn animals. Yowceph (Joseph) dropped the lead rope of Bil'am the donkey and grabbed the hand of his wife Miryam. As he held the small lantern up with his other hand he simply said, "Well, the fresh straw beats sleeping on the cold ground."

As they walked slowly closer to the center of the small cave so as not to alarm or frighten the barn animals, Miryam began to feel another contraction beginning to build. The contractions were becoming more frequent and more intense. She tried to take a deep breath and said, "I have to lie down. Please go see if the innkeeper's wife can come to help. The baby is not going to wait much longer!" Then she squeezed hard the hand of Yowceph as he stayed by her side offering words of comfort until the contraction was over. At the conclusion, he ran as fast as he could back to the front door and began knocking again. Ger'shom answered the door again and said, "What is it?" Yowceph (Joseph) out of breath answered, "Sir my wife needs your wife. The baby is coming!" Ger'shom summoned his wife and the pudgy little woman trotted to the cave with Yowceph following close behind her in the moonlight. She slung the crude gate open and ran to the side of Miryam. Yowceph closed the gate and joined the two women as the innkeeper's wife asked about the timing of the contractions and their intensity. After being satisfied with the information she received from Miryam, she named a list of items that Yowceph was to go back to the inn and get from her husband with the final instructions of, "Now be quick about it we don't have much time here!" Ger'shom gathered the requested items and helped Yowceph (Joseph) carry them to the cave. Then the innkeeper's wife instructed both men to leave the cave at once.

The innkeeper's wife gave her a thick wooden spoon to bite down on to help get through the final contractions. After a period of intense excruciating pain of labor the head of the baby had crowned and Miryam had the urge to push. She was exhausted but she pushed with all her remaining energy. Finally, on the third push Miryam (Mary) mustered all the energy and strength that she had left and with a big push………..

"Unseen Footsteps of Jesus"
OLAM
HABA
(Future World)
Jerry Ayers

"Unseen Footsteps of Jesus"
OLAM
HABA
(Future World)
Mysteries Book 2: "The Dawning"
Jerry Ayers

"Unseen Footsteps of Jesus"
OLAM
HABA
(Future World)
Jerry Ayers

"Unseen Footsteps of Jesus"
OLAM
HABA
(Future World)
Jerry Ayers

"Unseen Footsteps of Jesus"
OLAM
HABA
Jerry Ayers

"Unseen Footsteps of Jesus"
OLAM
HABA
(Future World)
Jerry Ayers

"Unseen Footsteps of Jesus"
OLAM
(Future World)
Jerry Ayers

OLAM
HABA
Future World
Jerry Ayers